YOUR SUCCESSFUL LIS CAREER
Planning your career, CVs, interviews and self-promotion

THE SUCCESSFUL LIS PROFESSIONAL | SERIES EDITOR Sheila Pantry

YOUR SUCCESSFUL LIS CAREER
Planning your career, CVs, interviews and self-promotion

Sheila Pantry OBE and Peter Griffiths

LIBRARY ASSOCIATION PUBLISHING
LONDON

© Sheila Pantry and Peter Griffiths 1999

Published by
Library Association Publishing
7 Ridgmount Street
London WC1E 7AE

Library Association Publishing is wholly owned by The Library Association.

First published 1999

British Library Cataloguing in Publication Data
A catalogue record for this book is available from the British Library.

ISBN 1-85604-329-0

Typeset in 11/14pt Aldine 721 by Library Association Publishing
Printed and made in Great Britain by Bookcraft (Bath) Ltd, Midsomer Norton, Somerset.

Contents

Series Editor's preface

With rapid technological advances and new freedoms, the workplace presents a dynamic and challenging environment. It is just these advances, however, that necessitate a versatile and adaptable workforce which appreciates that lifelong full-time jobs are a thing of the past. Work is being contracted out, de-structured organizations are emerging, and different skills and approaches are required from all workers who must solve new and changing problems. These workers must become self motivated, multi-skilled and constantly learn. Demonstrating the international economic importance of professional development, the European Commission has officially voiced its support for a European community committed to lifelong learning.

For the information professional, the key to success in this potentially destabilizing context is to develop the new skills the workplace demands. Above all, the LIS professional must actively prioritize a commitment to continuous professional development. The information industry is growing fast and the LIS profession is experiencing very rapid change. This series has been designed to help you manage change by ensuring the growth of your own portfolio of professional skills. By reading these books you will have begun the process of seeing yourself as your own best resource and accepting the rewarding challenge of staying ahead of the game.

The series is very practical, focusing on specific topics relevant to all types of library and information service. Recognizing that your time is precious, these books have been written so that they may be easily read and digested. They include instantly applicable ideas and techniques which you can put to the test in your own workplace, helping you to succeed in your job.

The authors have been selected because of their practical experience and enthusiasm for their chosen topic and we hope you will benefit from their advice and guidance. The points for reflection, checklists and summaries are designed to provide stepping stones for you to assess your understanding of the topic as you read.

In *Your successful LIS career*, Peter Griffiths and I demonstrate why it is vital for individual employees in the current job market to promote their own professional self-development and to be aware of the ways in which they can achieve this. The book is intended to provide guidance on managing every stage of a career - whether you are a young person considering a career in library and information science and wanting to know how to get a foot on the ladder after qualification, an information manager, specialist or librarian in mid-career, or even a candidate for more senior positions wanting to get a view of the current state of the profession as a whole.

Books in this series are intentionally short in length and are intended to help the busy professional, therefore they cannot deal with all these situations in great detail, but there are extensive lists of other information sources to allow the reader to follow up on any point.

We have drawn on our experience of many jobs and hope that the guidance offered will help all LIS professionals, whichever background they are working in. May I wish you enjoyment and satisfaction in your endeavours to successfully carve out and manage your information career!

Sheila Pantry, OBE

Foreword

If you are about to read this book then you are already on the right track to Your Successful LIS Career. It is very hard to know at the beginning of your working life what the future holds for you. You may have some ideas, you may have none. You may be quite certain about how you are going to progress. Those who are further down the track can look back and reflect on whether progress has been made as intended; whether things have been better or worse than planned and perhaps look at opportunities for moving forward in a positive or different manner.

One thing in the world of work is fairly certain. Few people (if any?) will still be doing the same thing in the same way they were doing it ten years ago or even last year. We should all have developed and kept our career moving. The changes in technology alone have ensured that.

It is vital to keep in touch with current job hunting techniques and to pay more than just lip service to continued professional development. There is no such thing as a perfect CV or application letter, nor is there a 'standard' form of interview. The minute a CV has been produced it will be out-of-date. It needs to be examined regularly and checked to make sure that it is always an accurate reflection of you and the skills you have to offer.

Keeping abreast of recruitment and selection issues is as important as keeping aware of current developments and issues in LIS. Just as the information society has created the necessity to add value to information, so must we as information professionals show that we can add value to an organization.

This book is an excellent guide to current thinking and provides an insight into many of the 'behind the scenes' aspects of recruitment and continuing professional development. Use it to dip into to in a quiet moment, take it on holiday and read it cover to cover so that you come back doubly energized or treat it as a valuable reference tool and refer to it when you need specific help. I will certainly be recommending it to the many candidates that I interview.

Sue Hill, MECI FIInfSc
Managing Director, Sue Hill Recruitment and Services Ltd

Chapter 1
Scene setting: the challenges of today's employment market

In this chapter we discuss:

➤ changes to the employment market in the UK and elsewhere
➤ the growth areas in employment for information professionals
➤ the changes and challenges ahead for the information professional
➤ the need to keep up with developments in education and training (continuous professional development)
➤ ways to acquire new management and specialist skills in order to be able to deliver the information services of the future.

Introduction

This book aims to demonstrate why it is vital for individual employees in the current job market to further their own professional self-development and to be aware of the ways in which they can achieve this. It is intended to provide guidance on managing every stage of a career – whether you are a young person considering a career in library and information science and wanting to know how to get a foot on the ladder after qualification, a librarian in mid-career, or even a candidate for more senior positions (perhaps with mentoring or careers advisory responsibilities) wanting to get a view of the current state of the profession as a whole. A book of this type cannot deal with all these topics in great detail, but there are extensive lists of information sources to allow the reader to follow up on any point.

This first chapter explains the importance of career planning and personal development for librarians and information specialists, and shows how their career patterns, expectations, and therefore the necessary preparations and actions differ from what was true as recently as ten years ago. Later chapters look in more depth at some of the overall issues of career planning, and in detail at some of the major events in a career.

We begin with an overview of the current state of the job market and look at the changing skills requirements for jobs with library and information science skills content. The sheer range of opportunities is wider than ever and presents problems for both employers and employees in understanding the implications.

People with other, often technical, skills are taking on the work that was once the preserve of the librarian. Looking in the opposite direction, librarians are finding their skills in demand in unexpected quarters of the computer industry as it gets to grips with the organization and retrieval of the information content of computer and documentation systems.

In Chapter 2 we talk more detail about the changes that are taking place and look at the various employment sectors to see what changes are taking place in each. The changes present a challenge to the traditional styles of career management that have seen many librarians through entire careers. Chapter 2 will also show you how to begin planning your own career, and indicate some of the elements that need to be taken into account as well as suggesting some ways to adapt to future changes.

Chapter 3 will look at ways to get a first step on the ladder, and some of the ways in which you can get practical help at all stages of your career. In the following chapters: 4, 5 and 6 we look at the process by which many jobs are filled, taking in turn job advertisements and applications, interview techniques, and the paths to further progress. In Chapter 7 we look at the wider opportunities to which library and information science skills can be the key, before the final chapter, Chapter 8 covers some of the many other questions you need to consider.

Employment patterns – no more 'jobs for life'?

In the late 1990s most people have discovered that there is no longer any such thing as a completely secure job. You cannot now expect to stay in a job throughout a career, or assume that your employer will chart a course for you through the organization. In reality, a truly 'glittering' career in information work needs careful planning , and nowadays this falls to you, even if your employer is among the good ones who include career development within their appraisal or personnel management processes.

On a wider scale, events on the other side of the world can now have a domino effect on jobs in any country; witness the downturn in jobs and redundancies resulting from the collapse of the economies in the Far East in 1998. As an information professional you are in a good position to be able to watch the events in the world through various information sources – newspapers, journals, media sources, and the Internet! – allowing you to track the impact of these events on your own sector of employment or interest. Your job could be changed out of recognition by events over which you have no control whatever.

Jobs also disappear. Those information professionals who have worked in the library automation industry, for example, are particularly aware that some of the largest companies, brand leaders of five or ten years ago, have disappeared and their staff have moved on or away.

The intensification of competition now forces many people to move into areas of work in which they may not have had previous experience. Senior staff are often fully occupied with their own jobs and are consequently too busy to be able to act as mentor or guide to less experienced people in the workplace. As a result each individual is constantly under pressure to keep the work flowing and to complete it as quickly as possible, often without the benefit of the full picture. Sound advice and development coaching are frequently lacking. The result is a stressed or 'burnt out' individual, without commitment to the employer, and someone who may no longer enjoy the work which previously gave him or her satisfaction.

Today, the customers of our information services have higher expectations than has ever been the case. As a result they impose even tighter deadlines, demand the use of a wider range of information sources and want the results to be delivered in a variety of formats in order to meet the effect of these same pressures on their own tasks. Fortunately, new information and communication technologies (ICT) have at the same time offered the information professional the opportunity both to acquire and to manipulate information more easily than in the past, although they have also given the customer the opportunity to make demands which force the information professional to keep abreast of the latest developments in these technologies.

In fact, librarians finally have the opportunities they have been dreaming of for decades. Their skills are being recognized by the wider world. 'Demand explodes for librarians with high-tech research skills' reads the headline to a story on this topic. It goes on to state that, librarians today are hired as 'high-tech wizards to navigate the Internet, establish intranets, search databases and classify information.'

The need for computer-literate librarians with 'stellar research skills' is growing rapidly. They need to grasp these opportunities (as we pointed out in *Becoming a successful intrapreneur*), but they also need to take these changes into account in considering and planning their future careers.

The effect of official policies

Changes in national and international policies are adding to the challenges that workplace technology has presented to information professionals. Many of the new proposals being put forward in the UK and across Europe will radically alter further the way information professionals in these countries work in future. Among them are:

- ➢ *New Library: the people's network*, published by the Library and Information Commission in 1997, and the follow-up report
- ➢ *Building the New Library*, which appeared in November 1998
- ➢ *The learning age: a renaissance for a new Britain*, which included the exciting National Grid for Learning initiative
- ➢ The UK Government's competitiveness white paper, which includes considerable detail on information and knowledge management issues in the main and supporting papers
- ➢ the European Commission's lifelong learning initiative.

These policies are just a few examples of strategies that aim to remove the divide between the information rich and the information poor, and reduce the consequent social exclusion. There are further examples to be found in many countries. Information is their common baseline, which presents challenges that the information industry must be constantly ready to accept. If not, other sectors will recognize the opportunities and take the lead, leaving the information industry lagging behind.

Knowledge management

The focus of many organizations on knowledge management shows, perhaps belatedly, how they are recognizing that the skills of information and library professionals match exactly what is required to organize, manage, produce and maintain information systems to enable these organizations to exploit their own knowledge base more fully.

As the discipline matures, the comment is increasingly heard that this is an area where librarians' skills are needed in order to bring order to the current chaos. Indexing, thesaurus management and other 'traditional' library techniques are being identified by information technology experts as necessary skills that are missing from their own strategies for dealing with information overload. Mainstream business literature such as Davenport and Prusak's *Working knowledge* sings the praises of librarians at some length. And this is just the latest in a line of such concerns in the business sector about information, knowledge, and the growing volumes of both that are being produced.

You cannot therefore assume that the nature or scope of the profession remains what it was when you entered it, and still less can you rely on the profession remaining the same throughout whatever length of career you intend to have in future. The pace of change is accelerating. Your choice is to manage your career and adapt to change (and the pace of change), or be sidelined. In a recent article to which we shall return later, one writer notes that you really cannot start a portfolio career in mid-career – it has to be planned and provided for as soon as possible after qualifying, not least because of the financial and pension planning concerns that arise. But if there is no alternative to changing job, starting your portfolio looks a better option than doing nothing at all.

The need for continuing professional development

For any information and library service to function effectively it must have appropriately trained staff. To ensure and maintain this position means first of all that a supply of new information and library professionals with these skills is required. However, it also means that the existing workforce must upgrade their skills to meet these new and constant challenges and opportunities in the information industry.

It may surprise people working in the information industry that of the 18,400 librarians and information scientists currently employed in the UK only 7,000 work in public libraries. Another 6,000 work in academic libraries and information services or schools, with the rest being deployed in a wide range of other organizations, such as financial, legal, consulting, engineering, and computing organizations, hospitals, national libraries, and government departments or agencies.

It has been said that one Sunday's edition of the *New York Times* today contains more information than a person acquired in a lifetime 100 years ago. The variety and depth of subject skills needed by information professionals therefore constantly need upgrading, as well as their professional competences. Without knowledge that is kept constantly abreast of that of the best informed of his or her customers, a library and information professional can do no more than run behind those customers. To provide a service that continues to play an irreplaceable part in supporting the organization's progress, the library and information professional must maintain an awareness of both subject and professional developments.

In the past many professionals felt that once they had gained their qualifications that was the last major effort they had to make. The wise ones realized that this was only the beginning and planned to ensure their continual professional development. The growth of a range of new styles of education and qualifications, such as the Master of Business Administration (MBA) or various courses offered by the Open University, have expanded the range available and many librarians have chosen to develop their qualifications and knowledge in this way. Others have acquired language or specialist legal skills that complement the requirements of their work. Our case studies examine various approaches to defining the skills that are needed by today's employers.

Three case studies of the range of library and information science skills

These examples, one from continuing education , one based on research, and one based on the stated requirements of employers themselves, illustrate the range of skills which are called for in candidates seeking library and information work in modern organizations.

Case study 1:   The EUROIEMASTERS Project

In 1996, a European Commission DGXIII project, the EUROIEMASTER, looked at the skills that were needed by organizations in the broad information industry, and at the same time asked these organizations to identify which skills would be needed to carry out jobs in a few years' time. Among the skills librarians have at present, the following were mentioned:

➢ managerial and organizational skills
➢ writing, including report writing, journalistic and editing skills
➢ presentation and communication skills
➢ publicity and public relations skills
➢ ability to operate a personal computer and general computer skills
➢ use of online and CD-ROMs and Internet usage, e.g. bulletin boards, e-mail, listservers etc.

Among the new skills mentioned by the organizations interviewed were these:

➢ knowledge and application of client/server architecture
➢ knowledge of software products and the ability to apply these at the client/server level

---

7

Case study 1 *continued*

➢ development of products, and marketing
➢ software, multimedia
➢ authoring skills, HTML and SGML skills (and now XML)
➢ marketing skills
➢ commercial focus skills
➢ knowledge management/information management
➢ knowledge of information content sources which are authoritative and validated
➢ financial skills/knowledge including costing
➢ language skills e.g. English, Spanish, perhaps Chinese and Japanese
➢ advanced communication and presentation skills
➢ interpersonal skills
➢ customer care skills – including the ability to understand what the customer wants.

Sandra Ward, in her address, in September 1998, as outgoing President of the Institute of Information Scientists also emphasized that the above skills should be acquired by information professionals. She made the point that many of these activities have been carried on by library and information specialists, perhaps using other names to describe them, for around half a century. The difference is that with the arrival of the information society, the value of the knowledge and skills of these specialists is being recognized properly for the first time. The potential for those now entering the profession is enormous, but they must acquire and maintain the necessary skills.

Case study 2: University of Sheffield public library workforce skills research project

A two-year British Library funded research study is currently being undertaken by the Department of Information Studies at the University of Sheffield to examine the requirements for and to help develop a public library workforce which can successfully meet these new challenges. The project will examine:

➢ employer needs and the curriculum
➢ factors which influence students' career choice
➢ recruitment and selection by employers
➢ retention of professional staff
➢ training and development
➢ career aspirations and opportunities
➢ leadership and succession planning.

This study, carried out by Richard Proctor and Bob Usherwood, will assess the factors encouraging staff to enter and leave the public library sector and the relative effectiveness of education programmes, and training and development activities. Through gaining an understanding of these factors, it should be possible to forecast future developments (for instance, as the New Library initiatives are implemented), and in turn to suggest the training and career development that will be useful to new and recent entrants to public libraries.

Case study 3: Employers' requirements in vacancy advertisements

In order to gain an impression of employers' requirements, we examined a random sample of 100 advertisements appearing in four issues between August and November 1998 of *Library and information appointments*, the former *Vacancies supplement* to the *Library Association record*. Vacancy notices for jobs at an initial or early professional level were analysed to determine what qualities or essential skills employers were specifying beyond professional qualifications or a degree in information and library science (or variant equivalent terms). Even allowing for some overlap between definitions of the terms most often recurring, which is reflected in the groupings commented upon below, the results were somewhat surprising. In particular, it was not library and information skills as such that were sought after.

Case study 3 *continued*

Ranked in order of importance, the competencies that employers specified were:

- communication skills (55%)
- IT or ICT skills (49%)
- management and organizational abilities (31%)
- teamwork or partnership skills (26%).
- related experience (26%)
- flexibility (22%)
- interpersonal skills (14%)
- existing knowledge of their subject or sector (13%, mostly legal libraries)
- knowledge of research methods and sources (18%)
- customer-related issues e.g. customer care, end-user training (17%)
- specific library skills – cataloguing and classification in particular (15%)
- ability to work under pressure and meet deadlines (10%)
- online or electronic publishing abilities (9%)
- languages (9%)
- self-motivation (9%)
- energy (8%)
- Internet authoring and coding (4%).

Training ability alone was little identified separately from customer relations. Perhaps surprisingly, specific recent skills that might be expected such as developed Internet skills (authoring and coding rather than searching) were wanted by only 4%, less than half of the 9% wanting language skills. (Two of the posts asked for Latin!)

Worryingly, 8% of the advertisements gave no useful information about what was wanted, providing only an overview of the employer's business. Around half of these were schools, giving rise to the suspicion that teaching staff or governors had placed these advertisements without any real understanding of what a school librarian should aim to do. (There were some good models from which they could have drawn among other advertisements, and good candidates would no doubt apply to those schools in preference.)

Case study 4 in Chapter 2 summarizes a similar exercise based on European advertisements.

A more detailed range of information will become available during 1999 from the skills and competencies research being undertaken by TFPL for the British Library, although this covers only the banking, pharmaceutical and information industries. Emerging findings suggest that important future skills will be those linking to the business goals of the organization – communication, marketing, business and social skills.

Other evidence is emerging at the time of writing from the Independent Review of Higher Education Pay and Conditions which is chaired by Sir Michael Bett and due to report in the first half of 1999. This suggests that some of the skills requirements we found in case study 3 may be in sufficiently short supply to affect the job market and therefore the prospects (positive or negative) of people interested in working in that sector.

Points on which to reflect:

➤ do you understand the challenges of employment changes in the UK and elsewhere, and can you identify the growth areas?

➤ can you foresee the changes and challenges ahead for the information professional?

➤ how do your skills match those that employers are asking for in current job advertisements?

➤ do you know why you need to keep up with developments in education and training (continuous professional development)?

➤ have you some ideas of the ways in which you can maintain this awareness?

➤ do you understand the importance of acquiring new skills, both information skills and general business skills such as marketing, to be able to deliver the information services of the future?

Chapter 2
Your master career plan or,
Do you have to kiss a lot of frogs to
find a prince or princess?

In this chapter you will find out:

➤ how to begin planning your career
➤ what types of jobs are currently available
➤ what is happening in the traditional sectors: public, academic and special libraries and information services
➤ what is happening in other sectors, including publishing, marketing, finance, legal, training and other types.

Do you really have to 'kiss a lot of frogs' to find a prince or princess? In other words, do you have to go continually in and out of jobs to find the one that really suits you at whatever stage of your career? We think not, and in this chapter show you how you can plan your future career – although, as we shall see in a moment, this is not to say that you can necessarily stay in one place forever.

The ... librarian is committed to lifelong learning and personal career planning.

[He or she] takes personal responsibility for long-term career planning and seeks opportunities for learning and enrichment. Maintains a strong sense of self-worth based on the achievement of a balanced set of evolving personal and professional goals.

Competences for special librarians of the 21st Century, 2.10

It is essential that you start to plan your career from the outset and continually assess where it is going or should be going. You must be able to take opportunities that come within reach where they suit your career plan. You can do this whether you have qualifications or are still working towards gaining them.

Job for life or portfolio career?

The idea that a single employer could offer a job for life in library and information work has taken a considerable pounding in recent years. In some cases, service reductions, company mergers or lack of funding have led to a fall in the number of posts and some redundancies. In others, staff have not been replaced and as a consequence the career openings in an organization have been reduced. Younger staff in particular have tired of waiting for 'dead men's shoes' and have gone outside the organization to gain further experience or recognition, and perhaps more rapid promotion.

So, while it is quite common to find that senior staff in larger organizations have worked their way up through the system – or at least, that they have spent their career in the same sector – there is a noticeable trend to the 'portfolio careers' of successive frequent job changes that are often found in sectors such as financial services or telecommunications. This trend has advantages and disadvantages for both employer and employee.

Staying with one employer demonstrates commitment but may restrict access to more senior positions as the career pyramid becomes narrower. A recent study of government librarians suggested that a range of factors affect the decision to apply (or not) for posts at the most senior levels, particularly whether the additional rewards are worth the extra effort and the challenge of acquiring the post.

As the current senior managers move towards retirement, the trend is in any case towards fixed term contracts – often renewable, it is true – rather than to open-ended appointments. There is likely to be more mobility among the rising generation of senior managers than has been the case until now, and certainly than was the case 30 or 40 years ago.

However, the departure of senior staff causes problems. It has obvious implications for an employer: not only the loss of the investment in the individual, but also, when a person defects to another employer following some kind of inducement, the loss of their knowledge and experience and especially their contacts to another organization. Given the role of many libraries in making neutral contact between competing organizations, allowing the mutual and beneficial exchange of information, the loss of the individual librarian's network of contacts can easily have a noticeable effect on the organization's competitive capacity.

But constant moves are still seen by many more traditional employers as a sign of insincerity and lack of loyalty, so the prospects for someone constantly on the move may be limited. In some areas these constant changes might even appear as a lack of commitment to the profession itself. The only consolation for an employer is that the short-stay employee will have little time in which to gather intelligence of use to a competitor. It can cause considerable problems for a project or a team that has been carefully welded together when a member suddenly decides to leave.

Risk assessment for jobs

Most people may think that risk assessment is all to do with working safely and healthily, but if you make it part of your everyday thinking and approach to work and life in general, it will provide you with a 'plus and 'minus' list which you can apply along your career path and which will help you in making other decisions.

Here is a simple risk assessment system with five basic steps – the 'AEIOU' model.

> *Assess:* What are the 'risks' or 'hazards' of the job: e.g. wrong management, wrong location, wrong kind of work for you in the near or middle-distant future. Ask your employer/manager or their representatives what they think of your prospects and skills. They may have noticed things which are not immediately obvious to you.
> *Evaluate:* Write down your findings (your plus and minus list). Your analysis of your future career will help to decide which way to

move. Either stay with the current job and seek opportunities/alternatives within the organization or take the initiative and try pastures new.

> *Improve:* Can these 'hazards' be improved or eliminated by negotiation – e.g. is it possible to change the terms of the job, so that you can gain some further relevant experience or be helped to obtain further qualifications such as an MBA, or are there any opportunities to work on projects which may give you a different type of work experience?

> *Observe:* Keep your written record for future reference or use: it can help you if you want to move at a later stage in your career. It will also remind you to keep an eye on particular areas for personal development or jobs which interest you.

> *Update:* As in all good risk assessment procedures, step 5 is to review your assessment and keep it up-to-date. If your organization has an annual appraisal system then you should revisit and update your plan before each yearly review. It will also show your employer that you are thinking about both your career and your work in the organization.

Is there a better job for you?

Even excellent jobs are vulnerable to unexpected risks such as business downturn. However, you can start to decide whether it is time to move to another employer or to devote your energies to improving your current post using a simple assessment. Consider the job and its prospects and class them on a simple five point scale as:

excellent – good – fair – awful – intolerable

If you rated your job as 'fair' or worse, your time is probably better spent on updating your CV, applying for other jobs and attending interviews. For 'excellent' or 'good' posts, it may well repay your effort to negotiate better conditions in your present post. Use this method to rate what you can discover about other jobs against your present one, and if you list and mark the elements which are important to you personally (colleagues, training, distance from home, etc.) you can make quite complex choices much easier.

Getting help

It is often useful to discuss your situation with someone else. At its simplest, someone, whether a professional or not, given a snapshot of your current situation may be able to help you sort out the possible options. Alternatively a mentor, either formally within the organization or informally among your circle of professional acquaintances, may be able to maintain a long-term watching brief over your career and apply detailed knowledge of your background to future oriented decision-making. In Chapter 3 we look at mentoring in more detail.

So what types of jobs are available?

Wherever there is an active organization, there is a need for information services. We both can vouch for the opportunities in a wide range of sectors: heavy engineering, iron and steel, research, mining, health, government departments and agencies, and public libraries; as well as consultancy working for many other clients.

If you are starting our in your career you may decide to gain experience in the so called 'traditional' sector of public and academic libraries.

Public libraries

Many public libraries have, sadly, been neglected or underfunded over recent years. Hours and services have been curtailed, bookstocks have been reduced and the status of the library in the community has declined. On the other hand you may find a public library which has taken an entrepreneurial approach and has expanded despite such constraints. Working in such a place would show you how to provide a wide range of public services, despite the need to generate a large percentage of the budget from income – experience that would stand you in good stead throughout your future career.

Working in a public library, especially a largish one with a number of departments, offers you opportunities to gain experience in a number of areas. These might include: reference, business information centres, children's libraries, mobile libraries, acquisitions, computer systems including Internet web services, as well as general lending library work.

Academic and further education libraries

Working in a university or further education library and information service will give you the opportunity to try out a number of different areas of work – specializing if you wish in certain subject areas, such as engineering or chemistry information. If your first degree is in these subjects then – coupled with your Masters in Information Science – they could provide an interesting career. The survey detailed in Case study 3 of Chapter 1 showed a substantial demand for subject knowledge or experience in professional posts suitable for those at early stages of their careers. Check a range of university further education prospectuses to see the range of subjects offered. A majority, if not all the universities have websites so you can quickly check the various faculties and the subjects they cover.

You will gain experience in teaching and coaching students, so your presentation skills will need to be improved; perhaps taking a course in these areas will help you.

Education and training sector

Do remember that schools, training organizations, training and enterprise councils and business links present opportunities for the library and information professional as well as universities and colleges.

Check the various directories, such as those published by CBD, which list associations, councils, boards and other bodies, and indicate which have information units. The British Library *Guide to libraries and information units* and the *Aslib directory of information sources in the UK* are other useful listings of libraries and information services.

The schools library sector has expanded considerably in recent years, to the point that many schools employ professional librarians who have considerable resources at their disposal. These posts are as likely to be advertised in local newspapers as in the professional press, and for a new post the specification may often be rather vague. Experience suggests

17

that when the a librarian in post moves on, there will be a detailed and ambitious job specification against which to pitch an application, reflecting the value of school libraries to their communities.

Work in a training body is likely either to support or form a direct part of the organization's services to its users. As such, this work may have a commercial element to it or at least demand skills in costing and charging for information services. This area of the education and training sector is still developing and opportunities will continue to present themselves. The role of many of these bodies in implementing official policies will stimulate their development.

Special information and library services

The special library sector is often overlooked as a career choice by newly qualified library and information professionals. The opportunities presented by working in a special library and information service are considerable. There you will find a wide range of subject backgrounds. Consulting the various directories and handbooks that cover the special information sector will reveal a plethora of organizations that have information services of varying sizes.

The satisfaction to be gained working in these specialist areas is enormous. Duties may range from building and maintaining a one (wo)man service, to running a large department within an organization which could be anything from a blue chip management consulting organization or financial house, to a pharmaceutical or chemical company. There are many opportunities to find interesting information jobs in less obvious industries such as the insurance and loss prevention sector, or the fire information sector.

Health libraries merit an entire volume to themselves and can encompass everything from patient libraries at one extreme to the heavy involvement of information professionals in the development of evidence-based practice at the other. The health sector includes the libraries and information services of locally, nationally and internationally funded public sector organizations, universities, charities, hospital libraries, private sector companies and their information services and products, government libraries, and parts of the national libraries. If you are working in a small unit you will find that Sue Lacey Bryant's *Personal professional development and the solo librarian* published by Library Association Publishing is a practical guide to identifying and meeting personal development needs.

Institutions

Many of the great and long established institutions provide their members with information services. They include the learned societies and professional bodies in the chemical, civil, structural, fire, electrical and electronic engineering professions; the professional organizations for health and safety practitioners and environment health professionals, the personnel and training institutions, and the registration and professional bodies for a wide range of medical, veterinary and related professions.

Don't forget that many established charities operate information services. Their range of subject coverage is also very wide, and many – from the Consumers Association to the various overseas development charities – undertake information research in considerable depth. Networking is often a very necessary feature of work in charities.

Government libraries and information services

Government libraries and information services form another considerable sector of work that remains unknown to some library and information professionals. Government departments and a growing number of government agencies offer superb opportunities to gain experience of work in a vast range of subjects. Each major department has a library service: the subject matter thus covers agriculture, health, health and safety, trade and industry, defence, communications, economics and finance, foreign affairs, justice, law and order, the environment, transport, taxation, and so on. The creation of the new assemblies and parliaments in Scotland and Wales will lead to an expansion of the roles of the Scottish and Welsh Offices that, subject to candidates meeting any language requirements which may be stipulated, will further widen the opportunities on offer.

Librarians in central government enjoy an increasing range of jobs, not only in traditional library and information work, but in a range of related areas such as managing and operating helplines and advice services, publishing and publications distribution, website publishing, intranet management, communications (both internal and external), business research and support, legal librarianship, and records and correspondence management. Information management and knowledge management roles are now beginning to appear. In many of these roles information professionals work alongside, manage and are managed by generalist or other specialist colleagues and their connection to the departmental or agency library is only through the head of the librarianship profession in the organization.

Local government offers a little-known type of information work in addition to public library service work in those authorities that employ information and library specialists in their administrative offices. Typical work includes providing information services for council members and officials, supporting the legal department, and maintaining and indexing official archives.

Law

The legal sector offers interesting opportunities for those wishing to work as a non-legal professional in the sector. In university law faculties, government departments and law firms the information professional will find a range of backgrounds, depending on the specialization of the organization (e.g. criminal law, company law, European law, tax law). A look at the membership of the British and Irish Association of Law Librarians (BIALL), or the European Information Association will reveal the different types of organizations in which interesting work can be found.

Finance and management and consulting houses

The skills of information professionals are increasingly appreciated in the financial management and consulting sectors. The jobs are demanding and exacting but the salaries and other benefits are considerable. Many of these organizations work at the leading edge both in their own work and in that of their clients. Many of the exciting developments in corporate intranets have taken place in the major international consultancy houses (particularly the so-called 'big six'). Information is the lifeblood of these consultancy firms, and information skills are valued within them. The major consulting and financial houses maintain offices not only in London, but in all the major British cities and many European financial and political capitals. The business language of most international consultancies is English, but good skills in a second European language are useful in this sector.

Publishing sector

Don't forget that publishing houses (including those involved in electronic publishing) may also have information services. Library and information skills have further applications in work such as maintaining information-based publications, proof-reading and editorial work. Knowledge of fields such as intellectual property, copyright and licensing can also be used in this sector and the organizations that support it.

Library supply: the book and IT trades

The library supply trades increasingly employ professional librarians. They may be recruited for their ability to verify information supplied by customers requesting publications and to maintain corporate information databases for book supply houses and publishers. Managers have found it cost-effective to bring librarians onto their own teams to liaise with library customers and to check the more obscure publication references. Those with information technology skills can find work as sales or support staff with library computer suppliers, making support contact with customers on a regular basis, providing training, or helping to deal with reports of problems. For those with editorial skills as well, technical writing of manuals or sales proposals is a further possibility.

Joining professional special interest groups

It is worth joining the various groups of The Library Association and the Institute of Information Scientists to find out more about the different sectors. You can attend meetings, go on visits to the information centres and libraries of the organizations, receive newsletters and other information which will give you an insight into the work of a particular sector. The same applies if your current employer is a member of an Aslib group. You may well read about or visit an information service that you would like to join, and you can save valuable time and effort by focusing your job searching on organizations with which you are already familiar through visits or reading.

Worldwide approach

Of course these opportunities do not stop at the frontiers or shoreline of your country.

In a guide such as this, we cannot cover in any detail the requirements for working in other countries. As a general rule, if you are a citizen of a member country of the European Union you can find work in similar organizations to those that we have described above. Your UK qualifications will be generally recognized (although their equivalence to other national standards will vary from country to country) under the directives on the equivalence of professional qualifications. However, just as in the UK, certain posts (for example in some government departments) may be restricted to nationals of the host country. You should check carefully before investing time and energy (and particularly travel expenses) in seeking work abroad. But for the right candidate a period working in another country's professional environment can give a career-long advantage in seeking further positions.

Case study 4: Working in Europe

The European Commission DGXIII EUROIEMASTERS project discussed in Case study 1 (Chapter 1) identified a wide range of skills as component parts of the Masters degree offered in Information Engineering. Among these were presentational, financial, management, project management, team-working ability and computer skills.

This suggests that many of the skills identified in Case study 3 (Chapter 1) apply equally well to posts elsewhere in Europe. In order to check this we carried out a further analysis in the same way as for Case study 3 on a smaller sample consisting of the 73 advertisements notifying vacant posts suitable for first or second professional appointments that appeared over the same period of time in *ADBS informations*, the monthly news bulletin of the ADBS, a French association for information and documentation professionals. Apart from the striking demand for good English language skills (62% of advertisements), many of the same requirements were present such as:

➢ team-working (34%)
➢ sector knowledge (27%)
➢ knowledge of sources and the sector (27%)
➢ inter-personal skills (14%).

The most striking differences were that the level of qualification required was frequently stated explicitly in terms of years of further education or higher degree (34%), and the number of posts requiring considerable previous experience (fully half, with 27% asking for two or more years in a comparable job, and a further 22% wanting at least one previous comparable job). Only 5%, half the proportion of the UK sample, mentioned the ability to work under pressure.

There was a relatively strong requirement for software knowledge and technical skills, often relating to specific non-Microsoft software, and some Macintosh and Unix computing. These technical skills were requested by 51% of advertisers with 14% wanting advanced IT skills.

Among the requirements largely absent from the UK advertisements were accuracy or a methodical approach (mentioned by 21% of French advertisers), and traits such as discretion and intellectual curiosity were listed as desirable qualities.

On the other hand, communications skills, which were mentioned by over half the British advertisers, featured only once in the French advertisements. Whilst many skills are indeed transferable, in

> Case study 4 *continued*
>
> France at least far more emphasis is placed on formal training and experience; the requirement for higher managerial qualities in this sector remains comparatively rare.
>
> If you are fluent in a second European language in addition to English, considerable opportunities are available. Even if your language skills are moderate, you might still be suitable for posts in some international organizations and colleges where the working language is English.

Outside Europe, documents such as the Special Libraries' Association's *Competences for special librarians of the 21st Century* indicate the skills that are considered essential in North America and other areas of the world where the American influence is strong. These are not explicitly ranked, but among the major professional skills identified are (once again): knowledge of database and information source content, subject knowledge, customer-related skills including training, and use of information technology; and among the personal qualities: communications skills, team-working skills, and flexibility.

It pays to research your target country's job market. If you decide to try for work abroad on your own account rather than through an exchange bureau, the best route is to contact one of the professional organizations in that country. Some of the UK organizations have links with their counterparts elsewhere, or you could find out from IFLA, FID or one of the other international professional bodies about the national member organizations in your chosen country. Alternatively – as we suggest in Chapter 4 – simply write to the personnel department of any organization for which you especially wish to work.

There are a number of websites that list job vacancies in particular countries, but you may need to be a member of the national professional society to get a password for the vacancy advertisements. Others such as the American Library Association site are open to all. Before you apply for anything, check your eligibility for the post and for residence and the requirements for visas and work permits. Contact the relevant foreign embassy or high commission in your own country for help.

To summarize:

After reading this chapter you should know:

➤ how the nature of work has changed from 'jobs for life' to 'portfolio careers'
➤ how to assess your current position and decide whether to move on
➤ where jobs are currently to be found
➤ whether your skills are transferable to other countries

Chapter 3
Starting your career

In this chapter you will find out:

➤ **how to research the marketplace**
➤ **where to find advertisements**
➤ **how to decide what is right for you**
➤ **how you can get some help on career choices**

We all know people who have very successful careers even though they have done no planning and have no real interest in finding their next job. They have neither the time nor the need for career planning. Most people are not as lucky as this, and need to spend some time planning an outline of their future career, and in reviewing that plan at stages throughout their career.

For a newcomer to the library and information profession, even before gaining any qualifications, the first step should be to find out what type of work is available and to bear your preferred type of work in mind when selecting suitable courses and options. In Chapter 2 we discussed the vast range of career opportunities in libraries and information centres in various sectors.

If you are still at school and thinking about a career in information and library work you should visit your local careers library or ask your careers adviser at school to give you relevant information about the opportunities available. Depending on where you live, it may be possible for you to visit information centres and libraries dealing in a range of subject areas.

Your local public library may well be a member of a local network that links public, special, academic and other libraries in the area to improve services to all their readers. More formal regional groupings of individual librarians are found in the branch structures of both The Library Association and the Institute of Information Scientists.

There are many ways in which you can gain an insight into the workings of a library and information service. You may for example find temporary employment in a suitable local service. Watch for advertisements in the local press, or call or write to some in your locality to offer your services using the directories listed at the end of this book.

Qualifications and training

The qualifications needed to be able to work at a professional level in the information industry in the UK are:

> first degree in any subject plus a postgraduate diploma or a master's degree in information science and/or library science from a recognized school of information science or librarianship
> a first degree in information science and/or library science from a recognized school of information science or librarianship.

In addition, some longer-standing members of the profession may have qualified after A-level studies only through one of two routes:

> Associateship of The Library Association following a two-year course in library science (postnominal letters ALA)
> Corporate (i.e. Full) Membership of the Institute of Information Scientists awarded on the basis of extensive practical professional experience (postnominal letters MIInfSc).

Neither of these options is now open as a practical route to qualification. Instead, members of each body make applications for the professional qualification by presenting evidence of professional maturity after a period of work experience in addition to the academic qualification that is an essential pre-requisite to a career.

Both The Library Association and the Institute of Information Scientists also award Fellowships (FLA and FIInfSc respectively) based on longer and more distinguished experience. (Aslib does not confer awards on individuals.)

Under the first draft proposals to merge The Library Association and the Institute of Information Scientists the new organization would have Chartered Member and Chartered Fellow categories that would equate to these professional qualifications, as well as other categories for new members and for honorary members.

There are a number of schools of information studies in the UK in a wide range of locations, including Aberdeen, Aberystwyth, and Birmingham, Brighton, Leeds, Liverpool, London, Loughborough, Manchester, Newcastle and Sheffield. Their prospectuses are available by post and increasingly in part or full on the Internet.

If you have a subject degree, working in a library or information service for a period will provide experience that will be of considerable use when you go on to take your diploma or masters degree in information science. Suitable posts for those intending to take postgraduate qualifications are often advertised in the professional press as well as in any advertisements that may appear locally. Even if you do not return to the subject of your degree after professional qualification, the experience will add to your employability.

S/NVQs (National Vocational Qualifications in England and Wales, Scottish Vocational Qualifications in Scotland) are competence-based awards based on workplace or training assessments of a range of professional and paraprofessional tasks. In the Information and Library Services field they are controlled by a Lead Body which also covers tourism and museum services. Although the higher level awards are not yet fully in place and there are few practitioners who have been assessed up to level 5, S/NVQs are proving a valuable career step for paraprofessional and other staff who aspire either to develop professional skills through higher awards, or who value the confirmation of their skills and knowledge provided by the awards at the middle levels (2,3 and 4). The awards can be 'mixed and matched' with credits from other relevant disciplines such as management and finance.

The professional bodies

Quite apart from the standard benefits of membership that we mention from time to time in this book, the professional organizations offer you some excellent opportunities to develop your career through becoming fully involved in their activities. All these activities depend on some kind of voluntary input, but they provide contacts, experience of working in teams and committees, experience of working with professional colleagues from other sectors and types of information and library services, and some exposure to the realities of commercial life if you work in the public sector. Members of this profession benefit from involvement with their fellow professionals in a way that few other professions do. This skill in networking has been one of the factors that has led corporate and public managements finally to recognize the value of their librarians and information professionals in new disciplines such as knowledge management.

Getting involved with one of the professional organizations is probably the most significant contribution you can make to your own career. If your employer already provides time in working hours for this activity, take advantage. If not, ask whether it is possible, and if the answer is still no, work out how much (or how little) it would cost you to devote one evening a month to your own career development. Then pick up that telephone and ask how you can get involved!

The current contact addresses for a range of the professional bodies and a note of some of their sub-groups are given in the notes for this chapter. At the time of writing exploratory work is going on to determine whether some kind of closer working or even merger of The Library Association and the Institute of Information Scientists would benefit the profession. Any change may well affect these branch and specialist group structures, so check for up-to-date information.

Specialist work

There are specialist groups working in many subject areas of librarianship. They include special interest groups of The Library Association, and the Institute of Information Scientists. Aslib, which has personal student membership, but is primarily an organization whose members are companies and corporate organizations, has a number of special interest groups based on industry sectors. They provide careers information suitable for school leavers as well as for new graduates and other university-level entrants to the profession. A number of specialist organizations serve particular types of library or subject fields. These include the Circle of State Librarians (for those working in government departments' and agencies' information centres and libraries), BIALL: the British and Irish Association of Law Librarians, AIOPI: the Association of Information Officers in the Pharmaceutical Industry, and IFM Healthcare: a sub-group of the Health Libraries Group of The Library Association, which focuses on information to support the management group in the National Health Service.

Where do I find out about available jobs?

Many advertisements for suitable posts appear in the 'obvious' places, that is the vacancy publications issued by the professional bodies in the library and information fields listed in the references to this chapter. However, probably as a continuing result of the publishing strikes in the *Times* group newspapers in the 1980s that prevented the printing of library job advertisements in the *Times Literary Supplement*, a range of other publications now carry advertisements for jobs in this field. The content of the publication may reflect the type of post; for example, the *Guardian* media supplement for jobs in publishing, newspapers and broadcasting, the *Times Education Supplement* and *Higher Education Supplement* for posts in schools, colleges and universities, and specialist trade magazines for their own sectors. Trade journals frequently carry vacancy notices too; for example the *Health Service Journal* frequently advertises jobs in health libraries in the NHS and elsewhere in the sector. It is worth remembering that personnel departments often do not know which publications carry library job advertisements, so an organization advertising a newly created librarian post may well restrict the advertisement to its own specialist trade press more out of lack of awareness than from any desire to restrict applications.

One of the best ways to find out what type of jobs exist is to check the various advertisements which appear in the Library Association *Library and information appointments,* which is issued twice a month to members and is also available on the Internet as *LA JobNet.* The Institute of Information Scientists and Aslib also have recruitment information sheets. Jobs are advertised by a wide range of organizations, so opportunities in all the types of library listed in Chapter 2 will probably occur over a short period.

Other advertisements appear in professional journals and newsletters, for example in *Information world review,* published by Learned Information, as well as various newspapers. There are a number of web-based recruitment services and posts are frequently advertised on the mailing and discussion lists operated by Mailbase such as lis-link.

You might also decide to apply for a job through an employment agency. A number of recruitment services and agencies specialize in posts in information and library services, and in a range of related work such as information management and knowledge management. The list of references associated with this chapter shows the main agencies in the United Kingdom. In a number of cases the agencies pre-screen candidates and then match and provide job seekers' details to prospective employers against job profiles. Some of these recruitment services will also give advice on the type of training, qualifications and skills that are needed for certain types of job, and advise on the range of posts and work available.

What recruiters want

Case study 3 in Chapter 1 looked at the qualities that advertisers are currently looking for. The stereotype librarian with a shy retiring personality will find it difficult to obtain a job in today's information industry because part of the job is being able to talk to customers, to find out what they want and to suggest ways to improve the customers' information. Librarians' computer skills must be backed up by the ability to discuss and teach these skills.

The generalist

Despite all we have said, you may find it difficult to choose a sector in which to work. In this case, you may do best to stay a generalist and choose posts accordingly. At the beginning of your career, public libraries can offer a wide range of work including business enquiries, music, local studies and work with children as well as the traditional adult lending and reference services. Generalist work is available in sometime surprising places: for example the Ministry of Defence operates some libraries for service personnel and their families serving at bases outside the UK; while many public library authorities operate service points within prisons, sometimes integrated with their own services, sometimes semi-autonomously, that offer library and information services to inmates. Generalist skills can, by definition, be applied in a wide range of situations and the choice of posts may finally be as wide as your imagination and enthusiasm allows it to be.

How long is long enough?

We all know people who say they have ten years' experience, but is it *really* ten years, or one year times ten? Those further on in a career will benefit from a change of work or job at three to four year intervals. (A year to learn a job, a year to do it well, a year to improve it and a year to get stale and find another job?) Too short a time and it is impossible to show any achievement or progress; too long a time and it looks like lack of ambition.

Some employers attempt to manage their employees' career development by rotating people and posts at regular intervals. However, it is quite difficult to do this at all effectively where there are very few librarians, or where there are only one or two senior posts. In this respect, some of the large universities, public libraries and industrial libraries score well. Conversely, with increasing specialism in areas of work such as internet editing (HTML coding and so on), people are less willing to leave posts that keep them at the leading edge, and employers are less willing to lose the continual application of skills that have been provided, often through expensive training.

You may consider staying with the organization for a second three- to four-year period if the job changes significantly or there are opportunities to learn other skills. There are moves in some areas of the civil service, for example, to create some kind of internal job market with posts occupied by people on a kind of informal limited term contract of, typically, three or four years with the employing section.

An employer may assist personal development by offering, for example, facilities to gain a further qualification such as an MBA, in order to retain the services of an experienced employee. The real question for the employee is whether he or she is gaining any more real and valuable experience by staying.

Work patterns

Other work patterns that may help both employer and employee to resolve some of these issues are also emerging. It is becoming more common for people to have two jobs, or to carry out their work on more than one site. (We shall be saying more in later chapters about related questions such as working from home and career breaks.) It is often possible to combine two or more part-time posts to make a full time working week. Providing that the law on working hours is not breached, the employee is clearly at liberty to combine posts into a longer week than a single employer might have provided. Such arrangements can provide a range of experience somewhat faster than a single job can do. However a potential employer would no doubt wish to ensure that there was no conflict of interest between his or her needs and those of the second employer and may place restrictions on other work, especially work intended to supplement a full time job.

Questions such as family responsibilities are clearly going to have an important effect on your need for and reaction to such arrangements. The literature suggests that working in a pattern outside the standard day makes many people feel exposed ('are they doing this as a favour?'), but it is worth bearing in mind that in some areas of the profession there is no such thing as a standard working day because the norm is to work shifts with days off midweek, when the library is often closed anyway.

In coming to decisions on issues like these a second opinion is often helpful. As we have already mentioned, a mentor can help you by providing advice of this kind.

Mentoring

Mentoring is an important activity that is often mentioned in connection with the career development of library and information professionals. It is a process that suits the profession well, and has particular benefit where a librarian or information officer is working in a small or one-person unit without access to other professionals in the organization. It allows a person to receive the benefit not only of the experience of another, but also of that person's experience in different sectors of information work. But what exactly is mentoring, and how do you set about doing it?

The definitions of mentoring vary. Research suggests a variety of approaches to the process depending on country, so that in the UK there may be more emphasis on learning and coaching, and less on sponsoring a person's entire career (which might, in the wrong circumstances, be construed as nepotism). Whatever else it is, it usually means the development of someone, usually younger and probably not within the same area of a management chain, who is less experienced in the profession than the mentor. However there is no 'right' or 'wrong' way to go about the process, as we shall see in the rest of this section.

A mentor is described as a trusted counsellor, guide, tutor or coach. (The term comes from the name of the friend of Odysseus to whom the education of Odysseus' son Telemachus was entrusted in the *Odyssey*.) The modern sense includes supporting and sometimes actively coaching a student in his or her learning, together with the idea of encouraging or even sponsoring and promoting the student within the organization or the profession. The rather ugly term 'mentee' is found meaning the person mentored, but the words 'protégé', 'learner' or 'pupil' are increasingly seen. Mentoring at its most effective ought to be a two-way process, so that the older person also gains benefit from learning about new developments and other points of view from younger members of the profession. It therefore benefits both parties and is good for the profession as it promotes a flow of ideas across the generations.

The relationship can be more or less formal, ranging for example, from occasional telephone discussions or lunch-time meetings, to more formal regularly scheduled meetings, probably in the mentor's office and workplace. Each of these styles has its advantages, with the more formal style probably approaching the that of a university tutorial session. This is more often found where an organization operates a formal programme of mentoring or personal development.

UK literature on the subject is in broad agreement about the features of mentoring. The summaries below reflect that tradition. Those interested in further aspects of mentoring would find it useful to read some US or other non-UK documents.

Some of the key elements of the mentoring relationship, according to UK tradition, are listed below. Mentoring should be:

> non-threatening and non-judgmental
> wider in scope than simply providing professional advice
> a long-term commitment or rather, agreement (but this is not to say that a mentor–pupil relationship that has run its course should not be replaced by another, or that either party can no longer take part in a useful mentoring relationship with other people)
> a commitment of time and energy by both parties
> an expression of mutual respect
> an introduction to other networks of people and influence.

Some of the elements of the mentor's job are:

> to manage the relationship – including making time for the pupil despite existing commitments
> to encourage and motivate, and to provide feedback
> to teach and to nurture
> to respect the pupil and his or her views, even when you disagree with them
> to be responsive to the pupil
> to consider how to provide a role model
> to demonstrate skills for the pupil to emulate
> to defend the pupil and provide emotional support where appropriate.

Some of the elements of the pupil's task are:

> ➤ to communicate ideas and reactions back to the mentor, failures as well as successes, and to discuss forthcoming areas of learning or development with the mentor
> ➤ to respect the views and advice of the mentor, even when you disagree with them
> ➤ to manage the relationship, including making time for the mentor and keeping to agreed appointments
> ➤ to keep interested parties aware of the relationship, within the bounds of confidentiality agreed with the mentor (this is especially important where the mentor is in a different management chain or even a different organization)
> ➤ to listen, particularly when the mentor is offering advice gained from his or her own experience on the avoidance of pitfalls.

Mentoring is a common and very valuable activity in information and library work. There are no formal programmes within the profession but many larger organizations have general schemes, and they can be found in other workplaces such as local authorities and public services. Some companies use mentoring as part of their general staff development. Consider whether your mentor need be a librarian at all. You could learn much, and also give much in return, if your mentor were a generalist manager, or a specialist in some other discipline.

The traditional networks that librarians and information specialists use to communicate provide the source for many mentoring partnerships. In a profession where there are so many small organizations and solo professionals within larger organizations, the contacts made at training courses, social events and meetings such as the members' days run by the various professional bodies are essential for professional development and to facilitate mentoring. Biddy Fisher's book *Mentoring*, published by Library Association Publishing, looks at mentoring from the particular viewpoint of libraries.

To summarize:

After reading this chapter you should know:

➤ how to find out about the different types of library where you could work
➤ what professional qualifications are available and how you go about obtaining them in the UK
➤ where to find recruitment advertisements, agencies and advice
➤ when to consider moving on
➤ some of the new ways of working (see also Chapter 6)
➤ how a mentor could help you.

Chapter 4
Applying for a job

In this chapter we reflect on how to go about seeking a job from advertisements, and other ways of seeking to enter the job market. We consider:

➢ how to find out about the organization and decide whether to apply
➢ whether to take a temporary post: their plus and minus points
➢ how to write an application letter and put together a CV
➢ competences: what are they and what use are they in job applications?
➢ what to include, and what not to include
➢ when to apply 'cold' for a job: the unsolicited job application.

How to read a job advertisement

We looked in Chapter 2 at the range of work that is now opening up for people with library and information science training, and in Chapter 3 at the places where you can find job advertisements.

It is already apparent that many suitable posts for librarians will not have the word 'library' or 'librarian' in the job title. It pays more than ever to begin with an open mind, and to read advertisements with this thought in mind: 'how do my LIS skills map onto the requirements of this post?'

Job advertisements give you two sorts of information: first about the jobs being offered and second about the organization. Sometimes you can glean as much from what the organization doesn't say, or how it says what it does, as from what it wants to tell you. Sometimes events have a way of catching up with an advertisement. A company may include a line about how well it is doing, when the newspaper stories say it has decided to lay off half its employees. A public sector body may be about to contract out its library. Each may still be a good place for a dynamic librarian to work, but it pays you to read around your application.

Most employers will describe a post in glowing terms and there will probably be an information pack or at least a more detailed job description that sets these glowing terms out in detail. There will often be a number of well-intentioned statements that declare the library to be some kind of paragon and the post to be vitally important in achieving this. If this is accompanied by a salary range that appears miserly in relation to the effort and skills demanded, it may be a sign of a future problem. It may be a fairly acceptable post for gaining experience but not for any long term future.

However you find your job vacancy, the same basic technique applies in applying for it.

Whether to apply for a post

The changes that we described in Chapter 1 have opened up a wide range of posts to librarians. Similarly, as a glance at the recruitment newsletters will readily show, progression and promotion are always taking place, and a good number of vacancies for qualified and qualifying information and library professionals is advertised in an average month. So the choice is wide, and all the reader need do is select the best paid posts and apply for them. Or is it as simple as that? Ask what position the job you identify will play in your career plan. Will it give you a skill you currently lack? Will it allow you to learn a subject area that you want to work in? Will it provide the next step on the ladder in your chosen area of work? Is the name of the employer going to make your future job applications look better? Or is it just a well-paid dead-end?

Salary will certainly be important, and if you are willing to take a salary cut to work in a particular library, you must consider the consequences carefully. (The interviewers will almost certainly remark on this, so think before you apply.) Fringe benefits may, if paid, make up for a salary drop. On the other hand, you may find the amount of pension contributions you now have to make has changed. Make sure you know what financial difference there will be overall if you are successful – and therefore what your bargaining points are if you have to negotiate on pay as part of the job offer when you are selected.

Do your homework

Find out enough about the organization to know that you want to apply. As a library and information professional you are in a unique position to find material about any potential employer. Read what it says in the advertisement, and see how they sell themselves. Find their annual report or any other publications, and see what they add, and whether they tally with the advertisement. If you can read a balance sheet, how is your prospective employer doing? What does the press say? Does the organization have a website? (Sometimes the opponents of the organization may have a website as well.)

If the organization manufactures something, look at its range of products. If it has a well-known person as chairman or managing director, find out about that person.

The result of this research will also allow you to give confident answers to interview questions such as 'Why do you want to work for us?' and 'What contribution can you make to this organization?' You will also become aware of any current issues that the interviewer may ask you about – or be able to steer the conversation round to show your awareness!

How to apply for a post

The basic rules in applying for a new post are extremely simple:

> ➤ always read the details carefully
> ➤ submit your application in the way requested by the advertisement.

If the advertisement tells you there is an application form, then obtain one quickly and complete it: you are likely to fall at the first hurdle if you simply submit your CV. (There is more about CVs later in this chapter.)

Similarly, if you are asked to submit a letter of application, this should be more just than a covering note stating the obvious fact that it encloses a CV. The letter must contain a statement of your reasons for wanting the post, and some idea of your aspirations and plans for the position.

Matching the employer's requirements

Clues to matching the employer's requirements are generally there in the advertisement, and in the application form too if there is one. You will be asked for a range of information, and that can suggest the points that the interviewers are looking for in making their first selection of candidates to call to interview. In Case study 3 in Chapter 1, we gave more detail about the kind of requirements that employers ask for in their advertisements, and warned against those who let you guess! This chapter is about how to make your application, so you will need to refer to the case study if you want to know more about the skills being asked for, rather than how to tailor your application to the employer's requirements.

Many jobs attract hundreds of candidates, and to make selection easier application forms frequently specify the format and order in which information should be presented. Selectors expect to find information in that order on the application forms they receive and will not look kindly on your application if it does not comply with their format. Increasingly frequently, the form has been designed to be scanned (by a person or even a machine) so sending your details in a different format will rule you out immediately. Again, if your application lacks information on a point that the employer considers important, it is more likely to be rejected. You only have a limited space in which to make an impression.

Fill the form with relevant detail, not waffle, to show how your experience matches the requirements of the post; your CV (see next section) will tell the chronological story. You need to ensure that the accompanying documents show how the experience there makes you the best person for the job. If you do not match the specification exactly but this is your dream job, you will have to make sure that you keep the selector's attention beyond the point that he or she discovers you lack one or more of the skills the employer wanted. But remember to be modest enough not to come across as pushy or arrogant. The employer might not have realized that a quality you possess was essential until your application pointed this out. You do not want to ruin the moment through arrogance!

Your CV

Even with an application form, you may be asked for your CV (curriculum vitae) or resume. This is a document which provides information about yourself, and most people are probably familiar with the basic concept. But a CV can be much more than this if you make it. It is your opportunity to market yourself to your new employer, so make sure that you do so!

Traditional CVs were simply list of jobs held with relevant dates when you worked there. Most employers ask for such CVs to be presented in reverse chronological order of post. This allows them to see the current or most recent job first and to read further if they wish. But it does not allow you to present yourself in the best light to the selector. You need the opportunity to show how your skills and experience match the demands of the job.

Some candidates therefore adopt what is known as a functional layout. This concentrates on giving information about the type of work that has been done, rather than the times at which it was done. This approach allows the candidate to group types of work together to show how he or she matches the requirements of the post being offered. For example:

Budgeting and management skills
Full responsibility to board of directors for library, managed budget of £xx,000 a year, (Widget Industries Ltd)

Staff management
Managed 3 staff (Widget Industries Ltd), managed one customer services assistant and one filing clerk (Worm Castings Ltd)

Professional skills
Online searching, marketing (Widget Industries Ltd), providing information to intranet service, SDI alerting service (Worm Castings Ltd)

It is an approach that has some drawbacks, quite apart from the obvious one that an employer will not welcome an application that is deliberately couched in a different way from the one requested. A functional CV:

> allows the candidate to describe the function rather than the title of the post, but that could be done in inflated, overblown language (what is the difference between 'customer service representative' and 'counter assistant'?)
> allows the candidate to group together similar jobs related to the post on offer, but that could disguise how long (or short) a time was spent in those jobs
> allows the candidate to show the range of work he or she has covered, and the development of skills, and also allows unaccounted time to disappear (don't be coy – if you took six months off visiting India, say so).

Because of these difficulties, some candidates present a 'combined approach' CV – that is, they give a functional analysis, which demonstrates that they have a strong claim on the job on offer, and then add a bare-bones chronological section.

Rather than just listing jobs, it is helpful to indicate major achievements in each post. Increasingly you will be specifically asked to list such achievements. An emerging approach is to list the competences that the candidate possesses and to use the job and training record to demonstrate these claims. A claim to hold project management skills might be illustrated by a list of project that the candidate has managed, or the ability to analyse computer software by details of work on a helpdesk.

Anne Applicant
Library Manager, Widget Industries Ltd, Borchester, 1996–date
Library Customer Services Manager, Worm Castings Ltd, Birmingham, 1993–6

Budgeting and management skills
Currently I have full responsibility to the board of directors for the library, and manage a budget of £xx,000 a year
Library automation project board manager (1997–8) – new system installed on time and below budget
Completed OU module in financial management (1996)

Staff management
Manage 3 staff (Widget Industries Ltd), managed one customer services assistant and one filing clerk (Worm Castings Ltd)
Library Association course on Managing difficult colleagues (1995)

Professional skills
Online searching, marketing (Widget Industries Ltd), providing information to intranet service, SDI alerting service (Worm Castings Ltd)
Trained Dialog Information Services user (1993, attended update meetings 1995, 1996, 1998)
Library Association course, Marketing your library service (1995)
Best Information Services course, Information for your intranet (1997)

Tailoring your CV to the post

You will probably need to fine-tune your CV to the post in question, if only to emphasize the appropriate skills you have to offer. If your technical skills include Unix and that is what the job needs, you need only refer briefly to your skills in other systems. If the employer wants to know if you can maintain the Unix web server as part of the job, he or she probably does not want to wade through your Windows NT management course certificates. Given the short time that the initial selector will spend looking at your application, if your relevant skills are not clearly visible in the first minute of reading, your application is unlikely to be successful.

If you are asked to complete an application form do not just submit your CV instead. If you are asked to submit a letter of application in your own handwriting, it is not sensible to send only a printed document of application. And make sure that that you provide the required number of referees.

Answer the questions on the application form honestly and be sure not to omit details that might prove troublesome at interview. Many people leave gaps in their employment record where they may have been out of work or have decided to take an extended holiday. Interviewers examine the information which each candidate supplies, and are perfectly capable of identifying unexplained gaps in candidates' details. (We mentioned above the problems of hiding this in a functional CV.)

If you were looking for work for several months, then include this information in your application. At worst it can provide you with something to discuss with the interviewer. (Keep a copy of what you put on the application form and take it with you to the interview.) Many interviewers are familiar with talking to candidates who have been looking for work, and will value your honesty rather than your deceit in concealing what is nowadays a common situation.

Be sure to give full details where requested on the form. Employers are now obliged to ask a number of questions relating to nationality and citizenship, and some of these may seem unnecessary or peculiar. Bear in mind that application forms are designed for use by a wide range of potential applicants, so do not jeopardize your own application by omitting details which you think must be perfectly obvious, or skipping those questions which you think are impertinent.

By the same token, be scrupulously honest if you are claiming guaranteed interviews, for example under the Disability Discrimination Act. Not only is it despicable to claim an interview by pretending to be disabled: it is also illegal, and you will be found out. If the Act does apply to you, make sure you get what is yours by right.

If you are in a post that involves 'having substantial access to children' – in the public library and school library sectors, for example – a further declaration will be required to ensure that you do not have any convictions or bindovers that could make you an unsuitable candidate.

Some forms ask for your full education history, others ask for your secondary or even your post secondary education details only. You may also be asked to provide this information, like your employment history, in a particular chronological order. Make sure that you comply with the request. If all the other candidates have provided their history in reverse chronological order, and yours begins with the earliest information, your form will be at a disadvantage. If you are asked for schools and colleges attended since age 14 or 16, do not include your primary school!

Awkward details

One of the most difficult sections of an application form to complete is one asking for your reason for leaving previous positions. In completing this section, you should provide information which does not raise doubts in the interviewer's mind. So do not denigrate your previous employers or colleagues. Remember that many interviewers will begin looking at candidates with an eye to their future career history, and will be seeking employees who will not go on to speak badly of their company or colleagues to some future potential employer.

Be particularly careful when describing the situation where you left a job for something better. Your potential employer will be wondering whether you will leave the new company too, should something more attractive come along. You need to present a career move in a positive fashion to allay this kind of fear. But many candidates' describe this situation by saying that their previous post gave no opportunity for promotion. This may indicate to an employer that the person may have an inflated view of their own potential or promotability, and they may be wary of employing them as a result.

Referees

You will almost certainly be asked to provide the names of referees when applying for professional posts, and often for paraprofessional positions too. Referees may well need to be people who have known you during your training and studies, especially if you are living in a new area whilst looking for work.

There are recent reports that employers are placing more emphasis on personal references as a way of distinguishing between a growing number of similarly qualified candidates. This emphasizes the importance of selecting a good referee – and of observing good manners. It is not only common courtesy to ask your referees' agreement before listing them, but it is also sound sense. People sometimes react badly to the discourtesy when finding that they are unexpectedly asked to provide a reference.

One of the authors remembers the reference provided by a distinguished elderly gentleman, his career in public and political service eventually rewarded by an appearance in the honours list, who found himself in this position. He simply wrote, 'I do not think Richard will actually steal anything from you.' Richard did not get the job.

Applying 'cold' for a job

It is often said that the best jobs are not advertised. They are filled by word of mouth, or by head-hunters employed to find candidates. This can happen with information service and library posts, although in some sectors such as the public services there are rules that preclude this kind of approach to filling many posts.

But what about the organization that you have set your heart on working for? Is it worth applying before a job has been advertised, or just in case – the library equivalent of cold calling? In many cases the answer is 'yes', although with some cautions. First, be ready for frequent rejection and letters telling you that any vacancies will be publicly advertised. Second, do not make yourself a nuisance. Try to discover whether unsolicited CVs are welcomed, or at least retained – and if so, for how long. Renew your claim when your previous application is likely to be weeded. Third, make sure the CV you send is explicitly tailored to the organization; if you are bothering them about a vacancy that may not yet even exist, then our rules about tailoring your application apply even more strongly. If your CV is badly targeted it will not get any attention.

But you may expect to get some benefit from a 'cold' application. At the very best, you could get a job working where you aimed to work. At the least you might have your CV on their file, or know their rules on advertising vacancies. When a job next arises, they may even remember your name and invite you to interview. Only make sure that the organization form a positive opinion of you.

Spoilt for choice?

At some points in your career you might hold more than one job offer. Which one will you go for?

Initially you must ask yourself 'which one do I truly want?' Money is not the only reason to pick a job, and indeed, as we saw above, it may be difficult to compare salaries. Which job comes nearest to your ideal? Do you want to stop working at weekends? Do you want to travel a shorter distance to work?

Other 'softer' factors are also important. Which looked the best place to work in? Could you face working with or for your interviewer? Did you like the feel of one organization more than another? Did the library seem friendly, or busy, or welcoming … or dirty?

If you find that you did not get the answers to these questions quite right this time, think through the process. If there needs to be a next time for job seeking, learn from the experience!

In Appendices 1 and 2 we have provided some sample documents to help you: a typical application form and a CV.

> **To summarize:**
>
> **After reading this chapter you should know:**
>
> ➤ how to apply for posts that interest you
> ➤ that research pays dividends
> ➤ what to include, and what not to include
> ➤ the role of referees
> ➤ that honesty is essential in applying for another job
> ➤ what to consider when choosing which offer to take.

Chapter 5
Your successful interview

In this chapter you will discover:

➤ how people reach interview
➤ what interviewers are looking for
➤ why appearances matter at a selection interview
➤ what kinds of interview there are and what other tests you might face
➤ what you can find out at the interview and what you should find out before
➤ what you should ask at interview (and what not to ask)
➤ how your behaviour can influence the outcome
➤ the 'do's' and 'don'ts' of recruitment interviews.

Interviews are for many people the most stressful part of their career development. What are they going to ask me? What are they looking for? Will they try to catch me out? It may be some comfort to remember that interviews are stressful for many interviewers too!

The techniques in this chapter will be suitable for both recruitment and promotion interviews.

Getting to the interview stage

In a moment we will describe some of the different forms of interview and other selection procedures. But some general comments on behaviour are in order first. The candidates for any kind of selection interview or test have been chosen on the basis of their presentation on paper, whether that is by application form, CV, or letter of application. They will have provided some standard information (age, education, qualifications, and so on) and a description of their career to date and perhaps their aspirations. Now that they have been invited to an interview they should have a sales pitch to sell themselves as the best candidate for the job. We looked at this process in detail in Chapter 4.

What interviewers are looking for

No interviewer wants to be the person who took on a square peg to fill a round hole in the organization. First and foremost, then, interviewers are looking for somebody who can meet their 'person specification' for the position and fit into the team and the organization at large. They have only a short time to make their choice, based on the interview, although you should have given them plenty of guidance in your application. They will be looking for someone who can communicate well with other people (especially the stranger conducting the interview), and in the case of information specialists they may well be looking for someone who can put across specialist and technical information in clear layperson terms. In a negative sort of way, interviewers are also looking for the awkward, ill-matched or difficult candidates in order to keep them out of the organization. Until the interview, the candidates are simply names and data on sheets of paper. The interviews put faces to that information and allow the interviewers to select the person (or persons) whom they think will fit best into their organization, both in terms of skills and of personality. Interviews give them only a short time to make their choice and give you only a short time to convey your message and your personality. Every second counts; so it will pay you to prepare well and think about how you are going to approach the interview to ensure you have your proper say.

Preparing for your interview

You cannot predict all the questions you will be asked in your interview, but you can make some intelligent guesses at the kinds of area likely to be covered. If you are being interviewed for a specialist post (such as cataloguer or research analyst) you could expect to be asked questions about these areas. Your skills should be taken for granted, based on the application you have submitted, and technical skills such as cataloguing are difficult to test in an interview. However, you could expect a practical test of some of these skills (for example, being asked to catalogue some items before or after your interview) and you are likely to be asked about the principles of analysis or current awareness, for example ('How would you go about choosing items for inclusion in a bulletin?'). Research your potential employers – and, if appropriate, their sector. Read their most recent annual report and notice which areas of their business they have highlighted. Discover what other interests, business or recreational, their senior figures have by consulting biographical directories. What do their competitors think is important? Have your potential employers been in the news lately? If they are a large company or a public body, they almost certainly have been. Even a small company may have made it into the local press, but at least find out what is important in their line of business and be ready to point to or comment on events in that sector.

Kinds of interview

An interview can take several forms. The form and structure of the interview will depend on the culture of the organization to which you are applying. You can expect a public sector body to be more formal about the conduct of an interview than a consultancy or a small business. But even this is not a hard and fast rule, as agencies and other areas of the public sector may adopt a more freewheeling approach which they see as being more commercially minded than holding a formal board, and small organizations may make their procedures more formal in order to ensure that they do not discriminate against any of the candidates.

There are likely to be some common features. One person or more will talk to you for something between 20 minutes and an hour, depending on the post being offered, and will record their impressions once you have left the room. At the end of the session they will try to put the candidates whom they have seen into an order of preference. In an organization employing a specialist recruiter, usually a personnel manager, the interview may be in two parts. The first part will be devoted to an exchange of information about your CV and what the organization or company has to offer. The second part may be with the manager who has the vacancy and who is obviously the one to impress with your information and library skills and knowledge.

For some jobs the interviewing process may run over several days or even weeks and the task of picking a winner or winners can be quite problematic in those circumstances. It is frustrating to the candidate and it is also frustrating and wasteful to the employer, as many good candidates will tire of waiting and take other offers. If you find yourself with a better offer, do tell the employer that you want to withdraw from the competition. It may make their task easier, and it will ensure that should you apply again you will not be remembered for your discourtesy. Conversely, many employers treat candidates with scant consideration, but unfortunately it is they who have the work to offer.

In the public sector especially, you may be interviewed by three or even more interviewers. The technique you will have to use is quite different from that needed in a one-to-one discussion, but such interviews have the balancing compensation that you will not be subject to the whim of a single interviewer whom you may fail to get on with, or who may know nothing about information and library work. In a panel interview, a chairperson (who may or may not be a specialist) will open the discussion, probably by asking some general questions about your career, or your interests and outside activities. Other panel members will then ask questions on professional issues, or on topical matters connected with the employer's business, or indeed on general political and social issues.

Other tests

Employers seem to be becoming increasingly fond of additional activities around the interview. In some cases, candidates spend a whole day at the employer's premises, and undergo a number of tests and visits, of which the formal interview is only part. Whilst this is nerve-wracking for many people, it has the compensation of giving a far more rounded view of candidates than a straight half-hour interview.

You may be asked to make a presentation on a topic of interest to your potential employer. This can take the form of a five or ten minute talk on a subject which has been notified to you a few days before your interview. You may be given an overhead projector or other audio visual equipment to use during the presentation. Ensure that you are able to use the equipment before you start. It is very distracting for your audience if you are constantly hunting for switches or trying to put your slides in order. Keep your presentation to the point and remember your audience's interests. Number your slides, make yourself a script, and follow it rather than trying to read from the slides. Once you have turned on the overhead projector, leave it switched on. The panel want to hear what your views are on the topic, not to know whether or not you can operate a switch. If the projector bulb burns out, that is a problem for someone else.

Some employers now use psychometric testing as a means of assessing candidates. You will be given either a sheet of questions with multiple choice answers, or perhaps a small machine like a calculator into which you enter your choices. After about 20 minutes, the paper is taken away and marks are allocated by trained assessors. There are no right or wrong answers to these tests, which is why some people think they have very limited value.

There are reports that some employers are starting to use more aggressive forms of these tests such as a new test called the Hogan Development Survey, which aims to identify poor behaviour when the candidate is under stress. Others use risk assessment methods alongside psychometric testing. Whatever your view, you will be very unfortunate if the selection of the successful candidate is based on the results of these tests alone. If they are used, it should only be to provide a better picture of the interviewee to complement selection interviews.

Watch your appearance

It is trite but very true that you only get one chance to make a first impression. If yours is awkward you will start your interview with a disadvantage. Start by being sure that your style of dress is appropriate. If your prospective employer runs a very formal organization, turning up in casual clothes is a very bad idea. (Jeans are probably a bad idea for most library and information work interviews anyway.) If the employer is in a more informal sector, then a more relaxed style is in order. However even in some traditionally unstuffy organizations, a surprisingly smart style is expected, especially among the professional groups. One good way of finding out the form is to ensure that you see the library before the day of the interview, and use the opportunity to observe the dress code of the organization.

Accessories rather than clothes often provide the chance to make a statement of individuality, such as perhaps a modern tie or scarf to lighten a plainer suit. Even here it is easy to make an error. A survey reported recently that men who wear ties decorated with cartoon characters come across as immature and having bad taste rather than a wacky sense of humour. In the same survey a large majority of managers thought that the choice of tie was an important factor in making first impressions and that unsuitable appearance at work lessened chances of promotion.

If you want to bring any paperwork with you do carry it in a smart file or briefcase, and please NOT in a plastic shopping bag. It might be as well to sort the documents within the file. Plastic files and dividers cost no more than a couple of pounds and can be highly effective. Remember you are trying to get a post as an information professional!

Jewellery should be carefully considered, and should complement rather than dominate your appearance. Some interviewers are still frightened by rings worn other than on fingers, or visibly pierced body parts other than earlobes. You can resume wearing such decorations once the job is yours, but on a first meeting you should restrict them to the minimum you feel to be true both to yourself and to your wish for employment. The same comment goes for hair worn in primary colours rather than the more traditional shades, or outside the accepted norms of length for either gender.

One of the many tipsheets for interviews suggests carrying an emergency kit in that smart briefcase, containing the following: moist tissues and facial tissues, a trial size mouthwash, cologne, a nailfile, brush/comb, personal business cards, two extra copies of your CV, a blank notepad together with a reliable pen (preferably one without an advertising slogan on it), Post-it notes, paper clips and sticky tape. (The tape doubles up for removing fluff from dark clothes). Female candidates are recommended to add spare hosiery if wearing a skirt.

Getting to the interview

You will probably be shown to your interview by an escort – a messenger or a member of staff. If a member of staff has been allocated to shepherd interviewees there may be the chance to overhear a little of what is of interest or concern that day, or for a few words with the 'minder'. The staff member may well be asked afterwards for any impressions of candidates, so it can do no harm and quite probably some good to be friendly and interested.

Making sure you get to the interview in good time will ensure that everybody you meet in the organization sees you at your best. Check where the nearest public transport or car park is, and be prepared for a traffic jam or for the tube to be closed when you calculate your travelling time. Use the spare time when you arrive to freshen up (using the content of your emergency kit) and be ready for the interview with a couple of deep breaths. Most organizations will nowadays expect that you had a cigarette (if you needed one) somewhere other than on their front step before you came in. Read anything relevant-looking in the waiting room but don't overload your memory. The contents of the magazine table will give another clue to the organization: do they put the latest current affairs and business sector magazines in the room, or the library's year-old discards?

Starting the interview

Take time to settle after you enter the interview room. This is when nervous candidates fall over furniture, or spill water jugs as they sit down. Approach the candidates' chair calmly, and use the time for the social pleasantries to assess your surroundings. In the time it takes the chairperson or interviewer to introduce the people in the room, you can check whether there is some water within reach, whether the chair is at a comfortable height (do not try to adjust it but note whether you are likely to have to control your fidgeting as a result), or whether you have encountered any of the interviewers before.

Interviewers will be looking for people who impress quickly as good team players with the ability to communicate easily and effectively. Establish comfortable eye contact: interviewers are frightened by people who clamp on an unrelenting stare, and are annoyed by candidates who look at the carpet, the light fittings and the furniture but not at the people they are talking to. An easy style (as close to a chat with another staff member as you can muster in the circumstances) allows you to look occasionally not only at the interviewer but also at any other panellists, ensuring that you spot any signs of puzzlement or boredom on their part – suggesting you need to explain more, or stick closer to the point.

Look to your body language. Use it to show interest and establish rapport with your interviewers. Curb your tendency to fiddle if that is what you do when nervous: leave your jewellery alone and keep your fingers away from your face. Use your hands to adopt listening postures, and show interest in what is being said as well as what is being asked. Lean slightly towards your interviewers without flopping onto the desk – a posture almost as bad as sliding back into the chair and collapsing slowly downwards as the interview progresses! If you are uncomfortable with your posture and the messages it conveys, look at a book on body language – but be sure to do it some time before your interview so you are not self-conscious about it on the big day. Be professional throughout and act maturely – curb any tendency to use childish gestures or behaviour. Think of the effect you are having on the interviewers and their perception of you as a professional person and potential colleague.

During your interview

The chairperson's introduction should allow you to relax into the interview, as far as that is possible! You may be asked a difficult question early on, so do not relax too much. It might be a trick question, although that really would be a case of bad chairing. However, if you really want to work for the organization that employs this chairperson, you will have to think on your feet and regard it as a sign of what is to come.

Sadly, many generalists in the chair of an information specialist board ask even the most senior candidates why they wanted to be librarians (rarely expressed, we find, in terms of why they chose the profession or the career). The best answer is to grin and bear this, perhaps prefacing the reply with an appropriate comment to the effect that this was a long time ago and the profession has developed enormously since that time. But if there is a truly intrusive question about your private or personal life, refuse firmly but politely to answer it.

You are likely to be asked early on why you want to work for this employer. This should not be a difficult question and you should prepare an honest answer in advance. You should have done some research about the employer as part of your preparations, so you should have much of the information to hand. Emphasize the positive qualities of your potential new employer and not the negative features of your current work. Focus on work issues rather than people problems. Never make slighting comments about your current employer – the interviewer will be thinking about what you might say about him in future.

After the 'warm-up' questions, usually covering previous career history and your qualifications, there will be a discussion that will cover things like your knowledge of professional issues of general interest and those that particularly affect the interviewer. You can expect a test of your knowledge and understanding of what the organization does, probably including questions designed to see if you share its values. There will also be questions designed to see how you manage and how you deal with everyday work situations. Always try to talk positively, in terms of what you have done, rather than theoretical answers that start 'First of all I would ...' and resemble the instructions for building a Blue Peter model.

Be prepared for members of the board to write things down, whether or not you are speaking to them at the time. The chairperson or single interviewer should be taking notes to ensure that all candidates have been given the same chance, and any other interviewers should be noting down comments on professional and other specialist matters. You should perhaps be more alarmed if nobody writes anything down during the entire interview.

Discussion of professional issues may prove difficult when there is only one specialist on a panel of generalists. This is particularly awkward when you are the first candidate at an interview session, because the laypeople (who will often include the chairperson) will not have had the time to start learning from candidates' answers. If you are a later candidate you could expect questions from the non-specialists based on their understanding of the answers of previous candidates, so there may then be misconceptions to correct with the gentlest of firm hands that you can manage!

Many candidates fail to impress because by this point they have become rather wooden. They answer without either engaging the interest or the attention of the interviewer, and fail to offer 'hooks' onto which further discussion can be hung. Closed answers, particularly those that consist of a simple 'yes' or 'no' with a minimum of extra content, offer no chance for the interview to become a dialogue and a discussion rather than an interrogation. Try to use open answers which invite further questions to which you already have the answers ready.

Interviewers despair when candidates use up all the prepared topics in the first five minutes. If you give short, unconsidered and undeveloped answers you may well find that after the first ten minutes the questioning becomes patchy and somewhat desperate. On the other hand, if you can achieve rapport with your interviewers in the available time, and make them feel they are learning from you, you are halfway home.

(The other half, of course, requires you to know what you are talking about.)

Wrapping up the interview

You will nearly always be asked if you have any questions, or further information to impart which you believe may assist you to get the job. Make sure your questions are real ones and show off your intelligence. If you believe that some vital information about yourself has not been covered either in your application form or in your other answers, then do add the extra information. Make it a crisp presentation.

Don't ask questions about the details of personnel policy (although it would be in order, for instance, to ask whether there is a flexible working hours system or hotdesking, this is not the moment to ask for a detailed account of the method used to run the system). On the other hand, if the situation is appropriate, you might want to ask what happened to create the vacancy. Did the last person get promoted, resign, take a career move or get sacked? The answer could be revealing, as could knowing whether there are any major new areas of work forthcoming or knowing about the organization's promotion policy and commitment to professional personal development. Remember that although the organization is asking the questions, they should be telling you enough to decide whether you want to work for them if they offer you the job. They will be saved expense as well as inconvenience if you find out at the interview that you could not bear to work for them, rather than after six months' induction training courses.

The chairperson will then formally bring the interview to a close, and should tell you when the results of the interviews will be sent to the candidates. If there is to be another set of interviews, then this information will also be given to you. The chairperson may shake your hand, so be prepared.

In some sectors it is the done thing to send the chairperson a note of thanks as a professional courtesy. If that is the case in your field of work, use the notepad in your emergency kit to note his or her name at some suitable point in the interview.

Make your exit as neatly as possible. Don't appear over-anxious to leave and do try to remember where the door is located – we have known interviewees who in their haste try to escape through a cupboard door!

To summarize:

In this chapter we have looked at many aspects of job interviews.

You should have some clear ideas about:
➤ how interviews are likely to be run (though there are always exceptions!)
➤ what interviewers will be looking for
➤ the kind of answers that will help the interview to go smoothly
➤ the importance of body language and unspoken behaviour
➤ what other assignments might form part of an interview
➤ what you can (and should) say at the end of an interview – and when to keep quiet.

The references for this chapter give just a taste of the reading material on interviews available. Entire books have been written on the topic. One last thought: when you have been interviewed a few times yourself, you will no doubt also have your own favourite tip. Why not exchange your tip for your colleagues' favourite interview tips, and widen your experience further?

Chapter 6
Next steps in your career

In this chapter we consider:

➤ going for another job in your organization
➤ going for promotion in your organization
➤ going for a better job somewhere else
➤ changing sectors
➤ working from home.

Going for another job in your own organization

Circumstances will determine whether you find yourself being moved from job to job within your organization. Larger employers will have a range of posts at most seniority levels within their organization and there should be some kind of planned management of staff development that will allow transfer between posts. This rotation will provide the opportunity to carry out a range of professional tasks within the information service and to develop a variety of skills.

In a small organization there is unlikely to be the flexibility to allow this. At best there may be a small number of posts at a similar level – usually the basic professional grade – where exchanges are possible. However you may find that you have to persuade unwilling colleagues to take on work in which they have little interest, and that the real opportunities are therefore limited. Another problem is that in a small information service, after you have done the other job, the only possible change is returning to your original job. The possibilities are therefore limited, and so quite probably is the long-term potential of the employer unless you are going to be content to do similar jobs in rotation for several years.

One alternative if you like your employer is to look for postings or secondment to other areas of the organization where you can either use your information skills or acquire other knowledge that will increase your value to the information service on your return. Librarians' ability to navigate information sources often makes them suitable for work in advisory roles and in customer service areas, where their training in dealing with people is an additional bonus. But the only limit is the bounds of your imagination, as a range of policy and case-working roles might be suitable. Research work might also be possible, making good use both of graduate subject-specialist knowledge and of information-seeking skills.

Reading another of our books in this series, *Becoming a successful intrapreneur,* may give you some ideas for lateral moves that could benefit your career, or suggest some areas in which you might want to work to acquire knowledge to use in your later career development.

If you find yourself reaching a dead end with your present employer, you have three realistic options if you wish to continue to be employed by someone else:

> ➤ going for a similar job with another employer
> ➤ going for a better job with another employer
> ➤ going for promotion with your current employer.

We shall look at each of these in turn and then at other work options later in this chapter.

Going for a similar job with another employer

If you have been doing very basic level work with your present employer, you will be able to apply confidently for posts doing similar work with other employers. The job listings that we considered in Chapter 3 will be your main source, although you might be able to obtain news of vacant jobs on the library grapevine. When you have been working for some time, the jobs that are increasingly advertised on the Mailbase mailing lists are likely to be of more interest to you than to the newly qualified librarian. Where the vacancy also appears in print, the mailing lists often have the advertisement first.

Before you apply, consider what you are looking for this time, now that you have some experience in employment. What are the good and bad features of your present employer? Carry out a SWOT analysis (listing *s*trengths *w*eaknesses *o*pportunities and *t*hreats) on your present post and see how they map onto the new post. The result could look something like this:

Strengths:	Weaknesses:
➤ good training policy ➤ good employee benefits ➤ twenty days leave a year ➤ Investor in People status ➤ good after-work social life.	➤ lack of progression ➤ poor physical surroundings ➤ poor catering and a long way from town.
Opportunities:	Threats:
➤ boss has six months to retirement and the post could be available ➤ entitlement to 10 training days each year ➤ chances to travel to conferences and make yourself better known.	➤ recession means funding is shaky and the library may be vulnerable ➤ IT section is making a stronger bid than library to run knowledge management.

This process will give you a clearer picture of whether and why you really want to leave your present post. Doing the same process using what you know about the second post and the employer will allow you to focus even more clearly on what you hope to gain, and whether the post on offer is the right one for you. You might in fact come to the conclusion that the right thing to do is to stay put until something better comes along.

Salary will clearly be a further influencing factor. It would be too mechanical and rigid to base your choice of post solely on allocating scores to each job and dividing the salary offered by that score, giving you a 'pounds per point' rating for the job. But it might be an interesting exercise, and could give you a final clue if you are finding it difficult to decide between competing offers. Consider that if the best-paid job available looks boring and has no prospects, it is probably not the best job on offer.

Going for promotion with your existing employer

Promotion with your existing employer is an option that is probably governed by practices peculiar to the organization. In some cases you may simply be selected for a vacancy and informed of your promotion. However, many organizations operate strictly controlled promotion boards, with advertisements placed through official channels inviting formal applications for the post. If you have any choice in whether to apply it would be useful to carry out the SWOT analysis in deciding whether to, before using the advice in Chapter 4 to help you to complete the application form.

When you go for internal promotion the situation is clearly different from when you go to another employer. The conditions of work, good or bad, are probably the same although the higher grade may gain some additional privileges or perks in return for additional responsibilities. The question of salary is likely to be out of your hands unless an open bidding system applies and you are therefore able to negotiate your new salary. On the other hand, your promotion prospects will have narrowed further and opportunities for suitable job swaps at the same level will have decreased, so in your medium-term career plan you should be considering how to find your next job even while you are learning the new one.

Another problem with internal promotion is that you often finish up supervising people you previously worked alongside and with whom you may have exchanged complaints about the management. Now you are expected to become one of those very people you used to criticize! In an internal promotion interview you are very likely to be asked a question about how you would handle this – especially if one of the other candidates is a colleague whom you would have to supervise in future. Everyone's answer is different, but your answer needs to be convincing – you need to prove, preferably from your own experience, that you can do it!

Going for a better job with another employer

A better job with another employer brings together the risk factors from both the previous options. On the negative side, you would be going through the stresses both of the more senior work and of the change of organization at the same time. Even if you are familiar with the type of organization, for example a council in the public sector, there can still be cultural and procedural differences between employers. You need to apply all the techniques we have discussed to be certain that the job in the new organization is a good career move, and that the organization itself is right for you. On the positive side, you will not have to manage former workmates, and there may be further opportunities with the new employer.

In all these cases it would be important for you to be able to demonstrate to your employer, present or potential, what value you have and what skills and versatility you can call on in your work. The best way of demonstrating this is through maintaining your CV – and presenting this in support. We looked at some different approaches to compiling a CV in Chapter 4.

You should also keep an up-to-date statement of your experience that can be brought into a suitable letter of application. In all but the smallest organizations you may be asked to make such a statement when applying for a post; even if it is not specifically requested, ask yourself whether it would be worthwhile including a suitable (short) supporting statement.

Referees

You will need to find referees who can provide a statement of support for your application. These will probably be requested on any application form that you are asked to fill in for a new job with a new employer. The application form will often specify the referees, for example you might have to list current or previous employers, or your university or college. The correct practice when naming an employer is generally to name the organization rather than an individual, who will in any case probably have to pass the letter to a central personnel office where records are kept. Where you do name someone you have worked with, make it clear when you are naming him or her in a personal capacity.

Seeking the permission of someone before you name them as a personal referee is a common courtesy that is far too often overlooked. Failing to do so risks the annoyance of your referee and consequently a less than flattering reference (see p. 47).

Be sure that your referees can speak between them for the range of your abilities. Academic and work referees will provide the detail of your abilities and suitability for the post in question. Personal referees can comment on your character and personality, but remember that they may be able to say little of your true professional skills.

Many organizations will save themselves the cost of obtaining references for every candidate for a post: some will only call for the references of short-listed candidates or even their final nominee, but they will probably call for your references at some time before appointing you. (They will normally respect your request not to contact an existing employer until a firm offer is being made.) So ensure that as full a picture as possible is given by the referees that you choose, and that what they have to say will match what you have written on the application form. If you think you will need your referees more than once, sort all this out before you make any applications.

It would finally do no harm to thank your referees, whether or not you are successful, in case you need to ask them again at some point. And if they have helped you get a better job, let them know that they have contributed to your success.

Finally, bear in mind that sometimes it is not only references that have to be taken up if you are offered a new job. Depending on the type of work, other checks may have to be made, such as security checks for some areas of government, and checks with various registers for work with children. It can take several weeks to complete these, so do not quit your current job until you are certain that they have all been successfully completed!

Changing sector

One simple statement can be made on this question. Changing employment sectors in library and information work can be difficult. But it can also allow you to build on your existing skills and to offer an employer the benefit of your knowledge in another sector. To achieve this may well require your full range of marketing skills. You need not only to sell yourself and your abilities, but also to put a positive spin on your desire to leave your current sector and start again in another kind of work.

Changing sector is easier at the early stages of a career. Certainly in the first years there may be a positive benefit in doing so if you want to progress to more senior levels. Subject knowledge is often a key; for example a law librarian could find work in any number of law firms, in the academic sector, or in government libraries, and so on. Health and medical libraries are another sector where the range of posts is widening as the skills of information professionals become better known, and mobility between types of library appears to be relatively simple.

On the other hand, transferring to an academic library at more senior levels without a long and relevant career record is uncommon. In some sectors, notably central government, the methods of recruitment preclude external candidates unless all internal avenues have been exhausted. Lack of experience in local government finance and management expertise would effectively prevent a candidate from transferring to the highest level posts in public libraries.

During local government reorganization, some posts were designated as available only to people already working in the sector, so as to protect existing careers. Were such events to happen again, you could find as people did then that the choice of posts suitable for a career change of sector becomes limited.

The best advice would be to try different sectors at the early stages of a career if you are uncertain where to make your progress. Go on visits organized by your professional body; organize work visits to your neighbours in other types of library. Then aim to develop the skills and knowledge (especially of financial and management procedures) that you need to reach the top of your chosen sector. You might also bear in mind that if you intend to go into consultancy at any point, knowledge of the range of library sectors will be useful.

Working from home

There are two possible reasons for working from home: first that you are working on your employer's business in your home for reasons of your or his convenience, and second that you are working as an independent worker on your own account. We shall be looking at becoming a fully independent consultant in a later chapter. But what if you decide to work from home whilst still employed, perhaps because of family commitments, or perhaps to reduce commuting?

In these days of advanced communications and technologies there is often no reason why some part of your work cannot be carried out from your home. There are many advantages to employers and employees in staff working from home, for some of the time at least. Among the possible benefits are:

➤ you can better concentrate on the work in hand
➤ there are fewer interruptions
➤ you have no travel time and consequently no daily exhaustion!
➤ you have time to explore ideas and carry out research.

Although it is clearly difficult for someone in a traditional library environment to work from home when the reference collection is 40 km away, it is quite feasible for someone engaged on research or electronic current awareness to do the work from their own sitting room or study and send the results to the main organization by fax or e-mail. Knowledge-based working is being increasingly quoted as a growth area for homeworking, and the possibilities were described recently by one commentator as being endless.

Among the disadvantages of homeworking quoted in a recent survey are some which militate against doing LIS work from home:

> ➢ lack of social contact
> ➢ lack of access to files
> ➢ difficulty in talking to colleagues
> ➢ difficulty in meeting colleagues and other people.

Interestingly, most of these disadvantages relate to contact with people: colleagues, customers, and social contacts. Modern communications make it far easier to make and maintain these contacts. So we suggest that if your work is mainly with electronic information sources that you access online and your customers are remote (telephone, e-mail or fax contacts), then you could probably work successfully at home if you can provide a suitable working environment.

In this case you should think about whether you can provide a separate work area in a part of your home. It needs adequate furniture (you will not work well at a rickety second-hand desk) and you should preferably have a separate telephone line. Consider where you are going to put papers and documents. Your employer may insist on doing a health and safety audit of your home to ensure that the working area meets the required standards.

Many people find that they work best by pretending to go to the office, sometimes by physically going out and coming back in, certainly by dressing in a businesslike manner, and often by doing something concrete like closing a door on the rest of the home when beginning work.

Some final words: make sure that you do not become the resident parcel collector for all your neighbours; think carefully if there is already a teleworker in your house – especially if you are the one who will make the coffee every time – and make sure you visit your base in the central workplace often enough to be remembered!

To summarize:

In this section we have looked at various options for moving on. You should have some ideas about these questions:

➤ is it time for your next move?
➤ do you want to stay with your present employer?
➤ what are the advantages and disadvantages of new employers for jobs at the same level?
➤ and for more senior jobs?
➤ could you work from home instead?

Chapter 7
Looking sideways ... and back

This chapter tells you about:

➤ other opportunities in your organization that may benefit your career
➤ opportunities from short term postings and secondments in your organization
➤ secondments outside your organization
➤ some options if your post disappears
➤ temporary and other short-term assignments
➤ going independent.

In the previous chapter we looked at the possibilities for developing your career by moving to permanent posts in other library and information services, and by continuing to do your present job from home. Now we look at the opportunities that can come from using your skills to do other kinds of work with your own employer or on loan to another. We also look at going fully independent and becoming self-employed.

Why looking at other opportunities in your organization may benefit your career

You may be surprised to read that we are suggesting that you may wish to move to other sections or departments within your current organization. Working in the information and library services affords you the opportunity to view the activities of the various sections within your organization, and you may be able to gain useful experience not available in your own area, e.g. finance or personnel. There may be opportunities to work on a specific project for a given period of time, or actually change jobs completely by, for example, working in the computer department, or moving into another department where information and computer skills would be of benefit.

The way to do this will depend on how your workplace is organized. You may need to enlist the support of the central personnel team. Be prepared to explain to others why your skills are relevant outside a library.

Short term postings

Short-term opportunities for other work can arise when colleagues are temporarily absent on a project or when a vacancy needs to be covered until a permanent replacement is available. There can be benefits for all in your offering to work for a short time secondment on another job like this. From a manager's point of view there is the advantage that you already have knowledge of the organization and how it functions, know the staff and can be useful almost at once in the new area of work. You can, at the same time, acquire new skills that are of long term benefit both to the organization and yourself. If you are covering a vacancy, you can see whether you want to apply for it on a permanent basis.

For example if your training officer goes on maternity leave, you could be a suitable candidate if your work has been involved with selecting training for your colleagues, or you can offer experience in organizing training events for your employer or your professional body. The opportunity to be involved in training would be a great advantage for you in your earlier career. As you progress, training knowledge becomes an important competence – whether as a manager with responsibilities for staff training, or as an individual wishing to continually progress your own professional development. Libraries are often involved with Investors in People, the implementation of S/NVQs, and specialist training. Another suitable secondment might be to a training centre, such as an open learning centre that makes extensive use of books, CD-ROMs, videotapes and other multimedia and audiovisual resources.

Some people are hesitant about leaving 'their' job for a secondment. There is a long track record in government library and information services of people who have been, in the jargon, 'outbedded' elsewhere in the department with great success.

Just some of the jobs that librarians have done successfully in public sector organizations in recent years are:

➤ senior financial manager
➤ managing a Minister's office in a government department
➤ minister's diary secretary in a government department
➤ advising on exports
➤ IT director
➤ contract manager for tendered services
➤ call centre service development manager
➤ records manager
➤ Internet editor, author and webmaster (a growing area of opportunities for librarians and information scientists)
➤ intranet manager (same comment as for Internet)
➤ chief executive's secretary
➤ public helpline personnel.

This is not to mention those senior figures in the world of public service, the arts, universities and so forth who have trained and practised as librarians!

The opportunities really are endless – and librarians' people skills, information management skills and IT skills make a winning combination.

Taking secondments outside your organization

Sometimes the opportunity may exist for staff to take secondments outside the organization. Your organization may have links with other businesses or institutions and by making your interest known, you could for instance, work in a charitable organization, or if you are in a government department or agency work with organizations linked with the particular government department's work. Sometimes it is possible to work in a developing country when on sabbatical leave, or to work with one of the international organizations such as the World Health Organization, the International Labour Office and the United Nations Environment Programme.

There are also opportunities for exchange of library and information staff through organizations such as LIBEX: Bureau for International Library Staff Exchange which is located at the Thomas Parry Library, University of Wales Aberystwyth.

A further alternative is Voluntary Service Overseas. Librarians are one of the categories of professionals that are urgently needed for work in developing countries across the world. VSO is a possibility both for young professionals at an early stage of their careers (for whom it makes a distinguishing feature of their CV) and for those at or near the end of a career, providing an opportunity to pass on their wisdom in a worthwhile fashion. The contact address for the current requirements is given in the references to this chapter.

If you have ideas about work elsewhere in the world you could also advertise for an exchange in one of the prominent library and information journals in the country of your choice, or contact the 'opposite number', i.e. the university library, public library or industry sector information centre.

Losing your job

In a guide that is primarily about developing your job, it is a rather sobering thought that people who thought they had a sound career suddenly find that their jobs have disappeared. We referred earlier to some of the possible reasons, such as global and local economic factors, mergers, downsizing and so on. None of the words makes it any easier, even if information professionals may be better placed than most to read the warnings in advance. A recent article includes the advice that you should remember it was your job that was made redundant, not you, and that particularly for older workers (which nowadays means those over 35) temporary work is probably the best way back into work. Dealing with redundancy is a subject on which a number of useful printed guides are available; for the information and library services sector guidance from the specialist library recruitment agencies listed in the notes to Chapter 4, or taking advice from someone to whom it has happened are two further ways of getting help.

Temporary work

Many librarians work for considerable periods of their careers as temporary staff. Indeed, some employers adopt a policy of offering permanent contracts to people who have performed satisfactorily on short-term appointments. And as we said above, doing temporary work is a way of returning to full-time work after leaving or losing another job. Being a temporary gives you some flexibility, such as being able to leave a bad job quickly. Be flexible yourself in return.

Temporary postings allow you to gain skills in different areas of work, since many employers will provide at least a basic level of training for temporary staff – who, after all, will be of little or no use if not trained, even if their departure is predictable, perhaps in a matter of months. Posts are also advertised on Internet mailing groups and web-based employment services. As we mentioned in Chapter 6, jobs often appear there before they appear in print.

Most of the employment agencies offer temporary work and it is a good way of finding out about work in different sectors before making a final decision on a career path. Talk to the agencies and see which one you feel most comfortable with. If someone asks you for money to find you a job, go to someone who doesn't charge candidates. There are plenty who don't.

Treat the agency like an employer. If you look a wreck when you go to the agency, they are unlikely to send you to see their blue chip clients. Take our tips on dress and attitude and apply them at all times. Tell the agency if you are going to be unavailable for work, for example if you are taking a holiday. They may have work at short notice and will need to know if you are out of the country for three weeks – the agencies also have a living to make and need to know who is available to fill assignments on their behalf. The other point here is that you may need to decide quickly whether you want an assignment – because if not the agency may offer it to the person who will get it if you vanish for a month to the Andes. Employers employ temporaries because they want their vacancies filled, not because they like paying agency fees!

Your employability as a temporary will be increased by possession of some basic skills, notably keyboarding and word-processing in one of the common word-processing packages. Knowledge of spreadsheets and presentation software will be further recommendations. Look to see whether your skills make you suitable for posts not only in mainstream information work but also as a web editor, knowledge officer, archivist or other related tasks.

Make sure that these skills appear on the CV you lodge with the agencies or the one that they help you to develop. Remember to update your CV as you gain further experience: you will obviously need to do so rather more frequently than someone in a permanent position. Use positive terms and highlight your achievements. (If you are going to be with an employer only for a short while, that employer would prefer you to make an impact during that time). The description will probably include a number of different jobs so you do not need to go to great detail about them: try to stick to a couple of pages unless you have exceptional experience to offer.

When you go to see an employer, you can probably ask more questions than we suggested were advisable in a permanent career interview. Get a feel for the place and whether you want to work there. And keep in the back of your mind the question as to whether you would want to stay there if the post suddenly became permanent.

Going independent – the pitfalls, perils and pleasures

Going independent is a major career step and you should not underestimate the seriousness of such a move. Nevertheless there is a thriving market in independent information and library work. The majority of independents describe themselves as 'consultants' but that can mean anything from being a freelance providing additional indexing from home, to being a fully fledged advisor on management and other practices in libraries and information units.

Many of the current independents chose to follow this path when faced with an unexpected (or – sometimes – planned) block in their expected career as an employee. Redundancy is a common and unfortunate reason for taking this path among younger people; older LIS professionals may find that after early retirement they can prolong their active careers through work as an independent.

You should also be aware that consultants are often called in to do jobs in cases when management does not want to get blood on its hands, so you may quite often be paid to say things that neither your temporary employer nor you find particularly pleasant. The article from *Program* cited in the references to this chapter describes a case study and it in turn refers to various helpful analyses of the role of consultants. Although now some years old, the analysis in Colin McIver's article remains pithy and to the point, with a welcome streak of humour throughout.

Much of the advice about working from home applies to work as an independent too – except of course that it is you who are now responsible for providing the wherewithal to operate the company. A concise guide such as this cannot set out in detail what you need to do. Advice from other professionals, such as accountants, is desirable, and as local rules will vary you should check with your local authority and others about the effect that using part of your house as working premises will have.

Space does not allow more than outline of how to make the decision to become self-employed, but firm answers to the following questions are essential:

➢ what do you have to offer?
➢ is there a market for your skills now and in the foreseeable future
➢ for how long can you survive without an income? It is not unusual for six months to elapse after start up before you receive any money.

Self employment really challenges people, and not everyone can succeed at it, for a whole variety of reasons. From experience we can give you some advice and guidance, and also some words of caution.

Setting up business

It is important when you start your business that you get the best possible advice from government organizations, your bank and an accountant. You can go to locally held courses run by the various governmental organizations such as Business Links, which help you in the start-up phase of your business. All the banks have excellent advice packages and can be quite useful in helping you to set up a successful information business. When business is really moving ensure that your invoices get paid on time, but remember it costs you in time to chase unpaid invoices. You need also to be aware that if you are involved in European Commission projects that you will have to wait to be paid for work that you may have carried out some months previously.

Keep a close watch on the state of your accounts. Your bank may offer online computer access to your accounts and this service would be worth having. Likewise an excellent accountant is a must: she or he will be able to save you far more money than you pay in fees.

Partners and associates

Be careful about the choice of partners and associates with whom you may join to carry out a piece of work. If they are not up to it, then your reputation will also suffer. Likewise, be careful about the type of organization or company you do business with, because it may be one that will not enhance your reputation. You may be desperate for a job, but do weigh up the pros and cons – would you be willing to work with an organization that you would not wish to show on your list of clients? These might, for example, be companies that are poor performers environmentally, or disregard the health and safety of their staff, or those that indulge in financial doubtfully behaviour.

Ensure equal division of workloads when working with a partner or partners, or you may finish up doing most of the work in your enthusiasm to get the job done well.

Equipment

Ensure that your equipment is robust, and that your telephones, answering and fax machines, and computer equipment are in good working order. Computer equipment must be Year 2000 compliant. If you are working to deadlines, the last thing you want is equipment that fails.

Keep a track on your consumables because the costs can soon add up, and ensure that your accountant knows how much you spend in these areas. However, much can be obtained free of charge at trade shows if you do not mind using other people's promotional materials as office notepads!

Likewise ensure that when sourcing overheads, such as your telephone service, that suppliers give you the best possible discounts. For example, many people's 'best friend' under British Telecom's discount schemes is their Internet service provider.

Don't forget that you will need to insure your equipment, as most domestic policies will not cover it, and that professional liability insurance will provide indemnity against claims for damages arising from your advice. Few companies offer this class of insurance, but both The Library Association and the Institute of Information Scientists offer access to tailored policies as a benefit of membership.

Re-using work

Keep copies of all your reports, both in paper and computerized format, because it is possible that some work can be re-used. Some organizations ask you to keep work for up to two years on your computer. However, ensure that the terms of your contracts do not prohibit you from drawing on previous work in this way.

Being independent, but working away

If your independent work takes you away from base, then do ensure that someone has access to your office and can retrieve information, receive and send faxes, deal with telephone calls, read e-mail and answer-machine messages and return them. It all is part of the customer care.

Extending your network and your skills

You must constantly extend your network by going to meetings, seminars and conferences. This goes for all information and library workers, but in particular for those working independently because 'seeing, being seen and talking' to other professionals are crucial to gaining future work. It is well known that over 80% of new work for small and medium enterprises comes from contacts and repeat orders.

Keep up-to-date with your professional development. Take every opportunity to extend your networks, for example into the wide range of offers of work that are available in Europe.

Getting the work

Obviously in a book of this size we cannot give you chapter and verse on how to get a continuous flow of work but when you are meeting a company representative always be well prepared and ready to act and think 'on your feet'. They may also want to extend discussions when they realize what you are capable of giving them as an informational professional.

When agreeing to a job ensure that the client organization's representative clearly understands:

➢ what they are getting for the price
➢ your day rate
➢ your expenses, including any hotels etc.
➢ the overheads involved – you may need to quote a percentage for administration costs.

When agreeing to a job, record these details in a contract. You could offer flexibility through a lower day rate if the job covers a long period of time.

The pleasures of independence

Working independently brings many pleasures. There are no bureaucratic interventions that take time and effort to deal with. There are no longer the regular unnecessary meetings that many organizations demand their staff attend. You can choose to work when you want to, when to stop and start, to work early or late in the day, or even at night! You can choose to have a holiday tagged onto a job, something that may be very difficult when working as a full time employee for an organization. Being self-disciplined is essential, particularly when you are solely responsible for getting a project finished on time.

Scott Adams, creator of the Dilbert cartoons, observes that independent consultants have often made a deliberate choice to follow this career path. They get to choose their colleagues, and do not have to carry out many of the personnel-related tasks that ensue from being an employee or a manager. Especially if they are working to supplement other income, they can reject unattractive assignments, or walk away from projects that are not earning their keep or are causing more stress than they are worth financially. (However, it would be as well to ensure you never want to go back to that company or sector if you do this other than by mutual agreement: word gets round.)

But the benefits of independent work include the freedom to think, to plan ahead, not to have to 'toe the party line', and to be able to move into other areas of work which may never be possible for an employee, learning all the time how to extend your services and expertise.

Working independently can be highly recommended for those with determination and grit who wish to continue from a successful information career in the public, academic, industrial or other sectors of information and library work.

To summarize:

After reading this chapter you should be able to consider:

➤ how you could gain experience outside standard working arrangements
➤ how you could work in a professional capacity on an exchange or as a volunteer
➤ how your professional skills could be used in other areas of work
➤ whether you have what it takes to be a successful independent professional.

Chapter 8
Other considerations in career planning

This chapter looks at a range of questions about your longer-term career. We ask:

➢ are you happy with what you are doing?
➢ what really interests or motivates you?
➢ how do you take your skills elsewhere?
➢ how do you follow the trends in pay?
➢ what other benefits are there?
➢ how can you return to work after a break?
➢ where do you want to be in three, five and ten years time?

We have shown you how to plan your career, assess the jobs on offer, apply successfully for a job or promotion and to look for other opportunities; we now ask: are you really happy and satisfied with your lot?

Do you get frustrated because:

➢ things don't happen as you would wish
➢ the pace of development is slow
➢ there are no real training opportunities
➢ there is no advancement in your career
➢ there is no 'buzz' about the place.

If you say 'often' or 'sometimes' to any of these, then it may be that you have been in your present job for too long and are literally marking time. You could be too comfortable but getting nowhere and lacking the sense that you are fully achieving what you really want to do. (See our advice on the duration of a job in Chapter 2.) But we do accept that some people just want to slip slowly into old age!

To help you out of this dilemma we are going to look at a number of factors which should influence you to think about whether and how to move on.

What really interests or motivates you?

It is no bad thing to want to try other areas of work. Indeed it is stimulating and challenging to spread your wings and move into other areas. We both have worked in a wide range of information services, starting in public libraries, so can really confirm these statements through personal experience. If you get bored with your daily work perhaps it is time to move on. This needs preparation. See the earlier chapters in this book, especially Chapter 2, to start you thinking.

Case study 5   New skills in electronic publishing

You enjoy using your IT skills and want to get more involved in other projects which will extend these skills. You may want to get involved in major initiatives such as establishing an intranet in order to get more experience. No doubt you have upgraded your IT skills so you can put together web pages. You will have improved other existing information skills such as your writing skills, e.g. producing press releases, summarizing documents, writing answers to frequently asked questions.

If not, then you might take relevant training at your local college or university if your organization is not geared up to providing the training in-house. Identify day or evening classes and make a proposal to the training officer. By doing this training you have established that you are in charge of your own development and career . You are also acquiring skills which you know are rare in your organization and this puts you at an advantage when the intranet is proposed.

In fact you can then propose the idea!

Trends in pay

If you are working in an organization that is not linked to any national or regional pay structures you need to keep an eye on the salaries and other benefits offered in the information sector.

The Institute of Information Scientists produce a regular Remuneration paper, which presents the results of a survey of the membership.

The Library Association also issues pay structure information with guidance for salaries in various types of library. This information is of growing value even in the public sector, where the old standardized pay scales are being replaced by more flexible arrangements. It is no longer true that you will be offered the same pay for the same job across the sector.

As our surveys demonstrated, you also need to look constantly at job advertisements, not only for information on salaries, but also for information about the skills required for different job specifications in the information sector.

Other benefits

Remember that pay is not the only thing to consider, and that any package offered may include health care, fees for training, generous holidays, insurance, pensions etc. Do look at the complete package. For instance, in some jobs, particularly in the electronic publishing industry, there are no company pension schemes, so what may seem a generous salary could be compensating for lack of pension. If you intend to move around you may want to consider a personal pension. Even if you intend to work in the public service throughout your career, different rules on contributions to the schemes in different parts of the sector make it difficult to compare salaries and conditions. It may seem far off, but do remember to look at such far off things as the age at which a pension starts to be paid!

There may be other benefits such as travel allowances, car mileage allowances, a staff restaurant at low costs, or Luncheon Vouchers. So when you are considering the package look to see how these other benefits add up and how (and whether) they will benefit you.

What lies over the fence?

If your interest is aroused but you have doubts about the upheaval that a job change may entail, such as moving house, do not be put off completely. You should satisfy your curiosity by at least measuring yourself against the market – read the advertisements, polish up your CV, and apply for a range of jobs in which you are interested. The response to the applications will tell you how you match up to requirements elsewhere and will put you in a position to decide whether:

➢ to take another job
➢ you need more training /development
➢ your present job is not so bad after all.

All this information at little or no cost !

Returning to work after a break

We want to give some words of encouragement to those who are considering returning to work after a break and are wondering just how they are going to cope with the job which seems to have changed beyond all recognition since their departure.

There are a range of reasons for being away from work. Most can be planned for at work – maternity leave, sabbaticals and in-service further education, for example can be written onto the planning calendar – but sometimes it is unplanned, such as long-term sick leave. We think the advice in this section is useful also for people being seconded to other organizations (see Chapter 7), and for people who get overseas postings as part of their career. In the rapidly changing world of work, even being away from the office for one year brings problems, but a three-year absence in an office with a different culture and climate can make a return to the home base seem daunting.

First we suggest that *before* any career break starts that arrangements are made for you to receive staff circulars or newsletters. If you are connected to e-mail from your home base it may be possible to arrange for you to be able to receive all this information through your computer, and to keep a record without gathering a heap of papers. This will keep you in touch with the ebb and flow of changes in your organization. You might consider doing some work from home, even on an emergency relief basis, particularly if you can meet any security or other checks that may be set.

You should try to keep in touch with your team leader and other members of staff about the developments in the services which are taking place. Ask to see major documents such as the specifications of a new system being brought into the information services during your career break.

Keep in touch, even to the extent of going on a training course. Ask if it is possible to spend a short period at the office every few months, if your circumstances allow this. If you worked as a one-person-band, ring the personnel office and ask them to update you on major events in the organization. If you are unpaid during your absence, remember the low cost of maintaining personal memberships of the professional bodies, and the news and information they bring.

Bear in mind that organizations (and their information services) alter track. Do a mini-audit of your employer before you go back to work. Once you have decided on the date of your return to work, try to visit the information service for a couple of 're-acquaintance' days, which will give you an appreciation of what is where, who is who (there are bound to be newcomers among the staff), and any changes to the nature of work. (The classic example is the arrival of the Internet – what would you have needed to do to catch up if you had started a five-year break as the Internet explosion was just starting?)

When you go back, don't panic ... remember that you have a lot of experience already; you will be surprised how quickly you get back into the swing of things. Remember, everyone feels the same after a long holiday!

Certainly there will need to be some adaptation on both sides. Ask yourself whether your habits have changed since you left. (Are you a late bird instead of an early one now? Will you need to leave early in the day to deal with family issues? If you have been ill, has it affected your ability to do any of your tasks?) You may need to take care that everyone in the office understands your circumstances, and that any changes to your work pattern are not seen as undue favours or as evidence of diminished performance. People may be looking actively for changes in your ways and knowledge, so you may find that you are in effect having to prove yourself to the team all over again. Remember, while you were away, someone else had to learn about your job and do it to something like your own standard. You now have to take it over again, and that will involve talking to the 'caretaker' to find out what has happened in your absence. You will need to exercise tact, as well as other interpersonal skills.

If you have been on long-term training, do not foist your new knowledge on everyone! Getting on with the job, and looking for an 'early win' by using your skills are far more effective ways of settling back than by going on at length about new theories and ideas. Harking back to your absence is not a good idea generally. Pass round the family photographs, tell people what it was like in a distant country, but don't make it the main point of your day. And try not to talk about your operation or list your health complaints twice a day!

If it helps, ask whether it is possible for you to work part-time, job-share or even work on a temporary basis to gain some further experience in a particular job area.

Flexibility

A quality commonly mentioned in job advertisements is flexibility. Now this may be no more than a euphemism for shift working; but it may also signal that the employer is willing to look at alternative ways of working which will avoid losing valuable trained staff because, for example, they have new family responsibilities, or because (as we saw in the last section) returning to work full-time after illness may present too great a burden at first.

Employers recognize that they have as much to gain as the employee by taking a flexible approach to these problems. Flexible working hours, part-time working, home working, provision of workplace crèches or job sharing are some of the ways in which the issues are being tackled.

Your manager (or you as a manager) will need to obtain agreement at senior levels in your organization to such changes, but this is becoming far easier to obtain than was the case even a few years ago. Fairness is essential, not least, for those areas where both flexibility and fairness are built into the law (such as on issues of disability); the system must be seen to be beyond reproach. Finally, the system must also allow employees to demonstrate that they are being equally fair and flexible – for example, by ensuring that they can be reached at all times when they are meant to be on duty.

Where do you want to be in three, five or even ten years time?

Depending on your age, you will give different answers to the above question. The answers will also depend on your total lifestyle and your quality-of-life requirements. We are reminded of the 35 year old who just wanted to finish work as soon as possible to do his own thing. At each appraisal he reiterated his desire, which he managed to achieve some 15 years later!

For those who are more career-minded we suggest that you should not hesitate to move jobs every three years or so. You may stay longer of course, if the job changes significantly or there are other compelling reasons.

So, finally where do you want to be in three, five or even ten years time? Your ideas should now be taking shape, particularly if you are keeping a really close watch on the leading edge developments that surround the information industry. Who would have thought that four years ago information people would be running their organization's intranet, or managing the corporate knowledge base? Being one step ahead of the game gives the information professional a certain advantage.

Now it's your decision

We hope that this book has been useful to you, whatever stage you are at in your career. We are sure, that armed with all this information, you will make the right decisions about your future career. We wish you luck and hope that you have as much enjoyment as we have had from our careers, which we still find as interesting and stimulating as ever.

Appendix 1
Typical questions on an application form

The form excerpts below show some typical questions that are found on an application form. Our comments point to common errors or loopholes in completing the application. Take care to ensure that your form is not ruled out or put to one side because you failed to do what was asked!

Application for Employment

Please complete this form in black ink or typescript and send it to the Personnel Manager at XYZ Co by the closing date shown in the advertisement. Please complete fully even if you send your CV as well.

> **Comment:** Do what is asked. Black ink and typescript allow the employer to photocopy the application. If you are asked to write a letter in your own handwriting, do not type. If you are asked to send a CV, do not just send a short letter that is not backed up by detail of your career and skills.

You will then be asked a number of questions (not shown here) that will include:

- ➤ your name (including any other names you have been known by)
- ➤ your permanent address and its telephone number
- ➤ the address and telephone number where you can be reached (e.g. during a summer holiday)
- ➤ your date of birth

> your place of birth
> your nationality (and probably your immigration status if born outside the European Economic Area)
> whether you have any disability.

Education after age 14
School, college or university, dates, examinations taken and results

> **Comment:** Note what is being asked for. Some forms ask for all schooling, some only for A-levels or degree level courses, depending on the level of the job. Examinations taken include the ones you failed! Remember that they appear on your certificates even if you obtained less than a C at GCSE or an E at A-level, so don't conceal them.

Employment information
Current or most recent employment
Name and address of employer; salary; dates of employment; type of work; reason for leaving

> **Comment:** Be honest. Be positive. 'Better job' is probably acceptable in most circumstances as a reason for leaving and is better than 'Argued with manager'. If you did argue, the reference will show this – but most employers will delay asking for a reference until after you have been offered the post, so you do not have to air your differences in public at this stage.

Previous employment
Name and address of employer: salary: dates of employment: type of work: reason for leaving

> **Comment:** The same comments as above apply . If you have

---

held many short-term posts, you may run out of space. Complete a continuation sheet; refer in less detail to temporary posts some time ago; if you were an agency temporary, ask the agency if you can quote them as a reference instead; or call the personnel office at your prospective employer and ask for guidance.

If you leave in detail about a post a long time ago (more than, say, 10 years) make sure it is relevant to the application. Make sure you enter details about the type of work, especially parts of it that seem to be relevant to what the new job involves.

Please say why you are applying for this post and what you think you can offer.

Comment: Write something; make it sensible. One of the most common reasons people give for any application is that the post is 'a challenge'. Concentrate on how the post matches your experience and skills, how it forms part of what you want to do in your career plan, and how you will bring skills, experience and enthusiasm.

You will usually get about a third to a half of a side of A4 paper for this section. Aim to fill the space without writing unusually small or large, and without writing anything unusually trite. Tell yourself that a machine could be reading your form before a human sees it, so your words should be positive and dynamic.

If you can't write anything sensible about the attractions of this job for you, and what you can offer, the chances are that it's the wrong job and you won't say enough to be selected for interview. Keep reading the vacancies listing.

Please give the names of two referees who can speak for your character, qualifications and experience. One of them should be your present or latest employer, if any.

> **Comment:** Once again, read the statement, as it varies from form to form. If you have to give your employer's details and do not want them to know, look for a box against the referee's details that reads 'May we contact them now? Yes/No' and mark it accordingly.

Please give any dates when you are unavailable for interview.

> **Comment:** Sometimes you can't help being unavailable, but you would be surprised how many people are called to interview on a day they forgot to tell the employer they were unavailable. We leave you to consider whether this goes down well with interviewers or not!

Please account for any time not otherwise shown on this form.

> **Comment:** It is crucial that you do not conceal anything in reply to this question. If you went backpacking to India, it gives you something to discuss. If you were ill, or even detained in a prison establishment, then this needs to be indicated, within the rules that apply on admitting spent convictions or patient confidentiality. If the reason for your absence from the job market is significant it can be taken up later. In any case, there is no possibility of an offer being withdrawn later if you are straightforward about such matters.

Please make any other statement that you wish in support of your application.

> **Comment:** Much as with statements to the police, you are not obliged to say anything but anything you do say may be used in evidence. So if you want to make a further statement about your knowledge, experience, or other matters, here is the place to do it. But if you are the kind of person who hates leaving blank spaces on forms, be sure that what you say warrants the effort both of saying it and of reading it.

Appendix 2
A possible CV for a library or information professional
(See also the alternatives in Chapter 4).

Anne Applicant	
Full name:	Anne Eager Applicant
Date of birth:	31 March 1972
Address:	28 Ambridge Road Borchester
Contact address:	10 Bull Close Ambridge
Telephone:	029 3034 2341
Fax:	029 3034 4312
e-mail:	annea@borset.gov.uk

- Don't write 'CV' at the top – it is unnecessary and some readers take exception to it.
- Give your full name as it will be needed if checks need to be carried out.
- If you have a name that is used by both sexes, you might head the CV 'Mr Hilary Applicant' or 'Ms Leslie Applicant.' The same goes for less usual first names. If you want to be very formal you could say 'Sex : Female' or 'Sex : Male'
- If you live at another address in the week, make sure the details are clear (and that you give a phone number where you will be!)
- Check your e-mail regularly!

Education
BA (Hons) 2:1 in English Literature, University of Birmingham, 1994
A-level: English (A), History (B), German (A)
9 GCSEs
MLib University of Central England, 1996

Experience
Borsetshire Library Service
Deputy librarian, Ambridge branch (1998 to date)
Graduate trainee, Borchester North branch (1997-1998)
Duties including lending and reference work, mobile library services and cataloguing.

Work experience
Library, Heavy Metalworks, Birmingham (1995)

Part-time employment
Checkout operator, Safeco supermarket, Borchester (1994)

- Give your academic history and professional studies. If you have an extensive career to present, you are unlikely to want to set out your GCSEs or O-levels in detail, or, perhaps, name your school. If you have an A-level in a language you claim to know, this would be useful to show in detail.

- List your experience in reverse chronological order. Employers' full addresses will be given if you fill out an application form, so save the reader's time here by giving brief details. Describe the duties in outline.
- Less detail is needed for early posts in an established career.
- Show other employment that reflects on your skills, eg working with the public as a supermarket employee.

Competences and skills Service to the public. Professional skills including cataloguing. Organizing training events	• Pitch these towards any pointers in the advertisement that ask for particular knowledge or experience. Here is the chance to set out your stand!
Languages German (fluent written, spoken and read)	• Make sure you really do speak these languages! Give some indication of how fluent you are and in what situations. If you have a second language (such as an ethnic minority language) as a mother tongue, make this clear.
Publications *Library services in the engineering industries of the Midlands* (Thesis, UCE, 1994, unpublished) 'Engineering libraries in the Ruhr', *International Library Student*, vol 1, no 3, 1997, pp 12-17	• Many people have a thesis to cite these days even if they are not prolific authors!
Interests Orchid growing, visiting National Trust properties, running marathons	• Make these interesting! It will not add much of value to your application to list 'reading' as a hobby – unless of course you specialise in a relevant type of literature
Referees:	• Only quote them if they have already agreed to provide a reference!

Appendix 3
Further reading

Chapter 1 Scene setting: the challenges of today's employment market

Abell, A., *The information professional of the 21st Century*, London, TFPL, 1997.

Circle of State Librarians, *Developing professionals in information work*, London, HMSO, 1992.

Various papers on professional development.

Circle of State Librarians, *Performance and potential of librarians*, London, HMSO, 1993.

Case study of training programmes in the Ministry of Defence.

Circle of State Librarians, *Time for change: threat or opportunity?* ed. P. Ryan, London, 1997.

Distributed by The Stationery Office.

Corrall, S., 'Defining professional competence: skills and prospects for the information profession', *State librarian*, Autumn 1998, 48–62.

Davenport, T. and Prusak, L., *Working knowledge: how organisations manage what they know*, Harvard Business School Press, 1998.

Department of Education and Employment, *The learning age: a renaissance for a new Britain, including the National Grid for Learning*, London, The Stationery Office Ltd., 1998.

Elkin, J. and Wilson, T., (eds.), *The education of library and information professionals in the United Kingdom*, UK, Mansell Publishing Ltd, 1997.

Fryer, R. H., *Learning for the Twenty-first Century*, London, Department of Education and Employment, 1997.

Golder, S., *Perceptions of the public library: a study of the impact on recruitment*, Submitted in partial fulfilment of the requirements for the degree of Master of Science in Information Management, University of Sheffield, 1996.

Griffiths, J.-M., 'The new information professional', *ASIS bulletin*, **24** (3), February/March 1998, (e-journal at <http://www.asis.org>)

Jones, B. and Sprague, M., 'Computers, change and the training challenge', *Personnel training and education*, **15** (3), Dec. 1998, 6–8.

Library and Information Commission, *New Library: the people's network*, London, Library and Information Commission, 1997.

Library and Information Commission, *Building the New Library*, London, Library and Information Commission, 1998.

Library and Information Statistics Unit, *LIST (Library & Information Statistics Tables) for the United Kingdom 1998*, compiled by Alison Murphy, Loughborough, LISU, 1998.

Library Association, *Framework for continuing professional development*, London, The Library Association.

Mackay, N., 'Technology, the public libraries network, and the need for joined-up thinking', *Journal of information science*, **25** (1), 1999, 1–6

Pantry, S., 'You and your career, or, Whose job is it anyway?', in Circle of State Librarians, *Effective library and information services in the '90s: 1993 Annual Study Day*, London, HMSO, 1994.

Pantry, S., 'Whither the information profession? Challenges and opportunities: the cultivation of information professionals for the new millennium', *Aslib proceedings*, **49** (6), June 1997, 170–2.

Riley, M., 'Trawling – swimming against the tide or going with the flow? Why are there so few applications for trawled posts?', *State librarian*, Autumn 1998, 7–14.

Shepherd, R., 'You just can't get the staff...', *Library Association record*, **101** (2), February 1999, 88–9.

Usherwood, R., 'Recruiting a first class workforce', *Library and information appointments (LA record* supplement), **1** (19), 11 September 1998, App. 377–8.

Ward, S., *Information professionals for the next millennium*, Presentation to Institute of Information Scientists Annual General Meeting & Members Day, 17 September 1998.

Ward, S., 'Educators, gatekeepers, advisers, explorers, organisers and engineers, analysts and assessors', *Inform*, **209**, November 1998, 12.

Wood, S. (ed.), *Continuous development; the path to improved performance*, Wimbledon, Institute of Personnel Management, 1988.

Chapter 2   Your master career plan: or, Do you have to kiss a lot of frogs to find a prince or princess?

Aslib handbook of special librarianship and information work., ed. A. Scammell, 7th edn, London, 1997.

Broughton, S., *The LION handbook: the library and information organizations and networks handbook*, London, Library Association Publishing, 1998.

British Library, *Guide to libraries and information units in government departments and other organisations*, 34th edn, London, British Library, 1998.

Burge, S., *Broken down by age and sex ; the career development of government librarians*, London, Library Association Government Libraries Group, 1995.

Carmel, M., 'Thriving amidst chaos: health care and library services in the 1990s', *New library world*, **26** (1120), 1995, 28–34

Centres, bureaux & research institutes the directory of UK concentrations of effort, information and expertise, Beckenham, Kent, CBD Research.

Councils, committees & boards including government agencies & authorities a handbook of advisory, consultative executive, regulatory & similar bodies in British public life, 10th edn, C. A. P. Henderson, Beckenham, Kent, CBD Research, 1998.

European Commission DGXIII, EUROIEMASTERS project brochure. Available from the European Commission DGXIII/E-4, Euroforum, 10 Rue Robert Stumper, L-2557 Luxembourg, Tel: +353 4301 34195 Fax:+352 4301 38069.

Hunter, C., 'Career patterns of librarians in government libraries', *Librarian career development*, **4** (1), 1996, 5–12.

Kirby, J, and others, *Empowering the information user*, London, Library Association Publishing, 1997.

Lacey Bryant, S., *Personal professional development and the solo librarian*, London, Library Association Publishing, 1995.

Lewis, N., 'Level 4 NVQs: an alternative route to professional status?', *Library Association record*, **101** (2), February 1999, 94–6.

Mackenzie, G., and Sturges, P. (eds.), *Librarianship and information work wordwide 1998*, East Grinstead, Bowker-Saur, 1998.

Meyriat, J., [Presentation in French of the European Project DECID: development of Eurocompetences for information and documentation], *IDT98 – textes des communications*, Paris, IDT / Jouve, 1998, 199–204.

Palmer, J., 'Skills for the millennium: the librarian of the 21st Century',: *Librarian career development*, **4** (1), 1996, 13–17.

Spiegelman, B. M., ed., *Competences for special librarians of the 21st Century*, USA, Special Libraries Association, 1997.

Thackray, B., 'National vocational qualifications in information and library services – how and why', in *IDT98 – textes des communications*, Paris, IDT / Jouve, 1998, 180–7.

Chapter 3   Starting your career

Mentoring

Clutterbuck, D., *Everyone needs a mentor: fostering talent at work*, 2nd edn, with research by Devine, M., and Beech, H., Institute of Personnel Management, 1995.

Fisher, B., *Mentoring*, London, Library Association Publishing, 1994.

Gibb, S., and Megginson, D., 'Inside corporate mentoring schemes; a new agenda of concerns', *Personnel review*, **1** (22), 40–54.

Levinson, H., *Mentoring: socialisation for leadership*, Academy of Management, 1979.

Megginson, D., and Clutterbuck, D., *Mentoring in action: a practical guide for managers*, London, Kogan Page, 1995.

Orth, C., 'The manager's role as coach and mentor', *Organisational dynamics*, 1987.

Pantry, S., 'Mentoring – is this for you?', *Information management report*, September 1995, 11–13.

Trott, N., *Mentoring*, Theydon Bois, College of Preceptors, 1990.

Employment agencies and advisory services, and their publications

(To dial the UK from outside the UK: international code is +44 and drop the first '0'; numbers starting 020 are available from June 1999 and replace 0171/0181 numbers from 22 April 2000)

Publications carrying advertisements for jobs

AIOPI newsletter, Association of Information Officers in the Pharmaceutical Industries
<http://www.aiopi.org.uk>
President: Christine Cameron, Elan Farmer Ltd
Tel: 01462 707282

BIALL newsletter, British and Irish Association of Law Librarians, Sue Frost, BIALL Administrator, 26 Myrton Crescent, Warwick CV34 6AQ, UK.
Tel: 01926 491717
e-mail: 106033.52@compuserve.com

Inform vacancies bulletin, Institute of Information Scientists, 44–45 Museum Street, London WC1A 1LY, UK.
Tel: 0171 831 8003/8633 (020 78.31.80.03, 78.31.86.33)
Fax: 0171 430 1270 (020 74.30.12.70)
e-mail iis@dial.pipex.com

Information world review, Learned Information Europe Ltd., Woodside, Hinksey Hill, Oxford OX1 5BE, UK.
Tel: 01865 38800
Fax: 01865 388056
<http://www.iwr.co.uk>

Library and information appointments, The Library Association, 7 Ridgmount Street, London WC1E 7AE, UK.
Tel: 0171 636 7543 (020 76.36.75.43)
Fax 0171 436 7218 (020 74.36.72.18)
<http://www.la-hq.org.uk>

Two issues per month.
Electronic version is called *LA JobNet*.
<http://jobnet.la-hq.org.uk/>
Prospects recruitment which is produced by DP Media in association with Aslib is issued as a supplement to Aslib's monthly *Managing information,* Aslib, Staple Hall, Stone House Court, London EC3A 7PB, UK
Tel: 0171 903 0000 (020 79.03.00.00)
Fax: 0171 903 0044 (020 79.03.00.44)
<http://www.aslib.co.uk/prospects/>
Aslib Special Interest Groups and regional branches are listed at <http://www.aslib.co.uk/sigs/>

Agencies

Birchs Consultancy, Warnford Court, 29 Throgmorton Street, London EC2N 2AT, UK.
Tel: 0171 588 5752 (020 75.88.57.52)
Fax: 0171 256 5501 (020 76.08.55.01)
e-mail: birchscon@aol.com
Capita RAS (Recruitment Advisory Services), Innovation Court, New Street, Basingstoke, Hampshire, RG21 7JB, UK.
Tel: 01325 745170
Fax: 01256 383786 or 383787
<http://www.rasnet.co.uk>
Glen Recruitment, Glen House, 200 Tottenham Court Road, London W1P 9LA, UK.
Tel: 0171 255 1139 (020 72.55.11.39)
Fax: 0171 436 4933 (020 74.36.49.33)
e-mail: glenrec@msn.com
Sue Hill Recruitment and Services Ltd, 71 Montpelier Road, London SE15 2HD, UK.
Tel: 0171 732 6671 (020 77.32.66.71)
Fax: 0171 732 6718 (020 77.32.67.18)
e-mail: <jobs@suehill.com>
<http://www.suehill.com>

INFOmatch, The Library Association, 7 Ridgmount Street, London
WC1E 7AE, UK.
Tel: 0171 636 7543 (020 76.36.75.43)
Fax: 0171 436 5843 (020 74.36.58.43)
e-mail: infomatch@la-hq.org.uk
<http://www.la-hq.org.uk/directory/jobs.html>

Instant Library Recruitment, 104b St John Street, London EC1M
4EH, UK.
Tel: 0171 608 1414 (020 76.08.14.14)
Fax: 0171 608 1038 (020 76.08.10.38)
e-mail: recruitment@instant-library.com
<http://www.instant-library.com>

LIBEX: Bureau for International Library Staff Exchange, Thomas
Parry Library, University of Wales, Aberystwyth, Llanbadarn
Fawr, Aberystwyth, Wales.
Tel: 01970 622 417
Fax: 01970 622 190

Recruit Media Informed, 20 Colebrook Row, London N1 8AP, UK.
Tel: 0171 704 6806 (020 77.04.68.06)
Fax: 0171 704 1370 (020 77.04.13.70)
e-mail: info@recruitmedia.co.uk
<http://www.recruitmedia.co.uk>

TFPL Recruitment, 17–18 Britton Street, London EC1M 5TL, UK.
Tel: 0171 251 5522 (020 72.51.55.22)
Fax: 0171 336 0605 (020 73.36.06.05)
e-mail: recruitment@tfpl.com
<http://www.tfpl.com>

Voluntary Services Overseas, 317 Putney Bridge Road, London SW15
2PN, UK.
Tel:0181 780 7200 (020 87.80.72.00)
Fax: 0181 780 7300 (020 87.80.73.00)
<http://www.vso.org.uk/contact/index.htm>
If you know the name of the person at VSO you wish to contact you
can send an email by following the format:
initialsurname@vso.org.uk

Others to contact:

enquiry@vso.org.uk	information on volunteerlng
Ibrooks@ vso.org.uk	for former volunteers
groups@vso.org.uk	join Local Groups
ekercher@vso.org.uk	join the Education Network
Ismith@vso org uk	join the Health Network

Chapter 4 Applying for a job

Abell, A. and Stenson, A., 'Building up a valuable career', *Library and information appointments*, 1 (14), 3 July 1998, 1–2.

Hill, S. J., 'Get that job – an introduction', *Librarian career development*, 3 (1), 1995, 5–8

'Hints and tips for getting that job', *Librarian career development*, 1 (2), 1993, 31–2.

Chapter 5 Your successful interview

Hill, S. J., 'Get that job – interviews', *Librarian career development*, 4 (1), 1996, 33–6

Lines, J., *30 minutes – before a job interview*, London, Kogan Page, 1997.

Peel, M., *Readymade interview questions*, 2nd edn, London, Kogan Page, 1996.

Wood, R., and Payne, T., *Competency based recruitment and selection: a practical guide*, Chichester, Wiley, 1998.
    A management book that describes the use of competencies and psychometrics in selection interviewing.

Dress and appearance

'Cartoon ties the limit for businesswomen', *The Times*, 1 January 1999, 3.

Bounds, W. and Lublin, J. S., 'Appearance still matters despite casual dress codes', *Wall Street Journal*, 29 July 1998, available at: <http://public.wsj.com/careers/resources/documents/19980729-bounds.htm>

Sampson, E., *The image factor*, London, Kogan Page, 1994.

Turner, L., *Looking good*, London, BBC, 1999.

Chapter 6 Next steps in your career

General

Adams, S., *The Dilbert future: thriving on stupidity in the 21st Century*, New York, HarperCollins, 1997.

'On track for the top.' *Information week*, **40** (7 October 1998), Careers section, 6.

Forrest, A., *Fifty ways to personal development*, London, Industrial Society, 1995.

Griffiths, P. D., and MacLachlan, E. A., 'Library consultancy in the Foreign and Commonwealth Office and the Overseas Development Administration', *Program*, **21** (2), April 1987, 91–107.

Hart, K., *Putting marketing ideas into action*, London, Library Association Publishing, 1998.

McDermott, E., 'Barriers to women's career progression in LIS', *Library management*, **19** (7), 1998, 416–20.

McDermott, E., 'A niceness of librarians: attitudinal barriers to career progression', *Library management*, **19** (8), 1998, 453–8.

McIver, C., 'Use and abuse of consultants', *Management today*, February 1986, 72–4.

Reeves, T., *Managing effectively. Developing yourself through experience*, London, Butterworth Heinemann, 1994.

Teleworking

Bredin, A., *The virtual office survival handbook: what telecommuters and entrepreneurs need to succeed in today's non-traditional workplace*, USA, Wiley, 1996.

Gray, M., Hodson, N., and Gordon, G., *Teleworking explained*, Chichester, Wiley, 1993.

Jervis, G, 'Health and safety in the home office', *Flexible working*, February 1996, 26–7, 39.

Johnson, M., *Teleworking … in brief*, Oxford, Butterworth Heinemann, 1997.

Kinsman, F., *The telecommuters*, Chichester, Wiley, 1987.

Mawson, A., and Tye, A., 'Practicalities of the office at home', *Flexible working*, November 1995, 36–7

Reid, A., *Teleworking; a guide to good practice*, Manchester, NCC/Blackwell, 1994.

Shaw, L., *Telecommute! Go to work without leaving home*, Chichester, Wiley, 1996.

Websites

Excite careers <http://www.excite.com/careers/>

Career WSJ (Wall Street Journal) <http://public.wsj.com/careers/>

The emergency kit is one of a series of hints contained in:

Hicks, R., *Interviewing do's and don'ts*, 1997.

<http://www.excite.com/careers/career_hub/manage/dodonts>

Lowri Turner (see references on dress) also develops the idea.

Chapter 7 Looking sideways ... and back

Dewar, D., 'Shock tactics for the job jungle', *Library Association record*, **100** (12), December 1998, 651.

Hannabus, S., 'Flexible jobs: changing patterns in information and library work', *New library world*, **99** (141), 1998, 104–11.

Weaver-Mayers, R., *'If you can't go......grow!'*, papers presented at the ALA Annual Conference, New Orleans, 1993, *Library administration and management*, **9** (1), 1994, 12–26.

Practical ways to cope with a career plateau.

Chapter 8 Other considerations in career planning

Biddescombe, R., *Training for IT*, London, Library Association Publishing, 1997.

Burch, G., *Go it alone! The streetwise secrets of self-employment*, London, Thorsons, 1997.

Foster, A., 'Knowing the business: knowledge professionals need more than information skills', *Information world review*, November 1998, 42.

Goulding, A., and Kerslake, E., *Training for part-time and temporary workers*, London, Library Association Publishing, 1997.

Morris, B., *First steps in management*, London, Library Association Publishing, 1996.

Morris, B., *Training and development for women*, London, Library Association Publishing, 1993.

Owen, T., *Success at the enquiry desk*, 2nd rev. edn, London, Library Association Publishing, 1998

Pantry, S., and Griffiths, P., *Becoming a successful intrapreneur: a practical guide to creating an innovative information service*, London, Library Association Publishing, 1998.

Appendix 4
Other organizations cited

ADBS, L'association des professionnels de l'information et de la documentation, 25 rue Claude Tillier, 75012 Paris, France.
Tel: +33 (0)1 43 72 25 25
Fax: +33 (0)1 43 72 30 41
e-mail: adbs@adbs.fr
<http://www.adbs.fr>

American Library Association, 50 E. Huron, Chicago, IL 60611, USA.
Tel: +1 (312) 944 2641 (1-800-545-2433)
Fax: +1 (312) 440 9374
e-mail: ala@ala.org
<http://www.ala.org>

Circle of State Librarians, c/o Membership Secretary, Ms H. O'Flynn, Department of Trade and Industry, 1 Victoria Street, London, SW1H 0ET, UK.

FID (Fédération Internationale de Documentation), POB 90402, 2509 LK The Hague, Netherlands.
Tel: +31 70 314 0671
Fax: +31 70 314 0667
e-mail fid@python.konbib.nl
<http://fid.conicyt.cl:8000/>

IFLA (International Federation of Library Associations), POB 95312, 2509 CH The Hague, Netherlands.
Tel: +31 70 314 0884
Fax: +31 70 383 4827
e-mail IFLANET@ifla.org
<http://www.ifla.org>

IFM Healthcare, P.O. Box 505, Maidstone, Kent, ME15 9PZ, UK.
< http://www.la-hq.org.uk/groups/hlg/ifm.html>

Special Libraries Association, 1700 Eighteenth St NW, Washington CD 20009-2514, USA.

Tel: +1 (202) 234 4700
Fax: +1 (202) 265 9317
e-mail sla@sla.org
<http://www.sla.org>

For other organizations of interest see:
http://www.la-hq.org.uk/directory/orgs_liaison.html

Index